# U.S. ARMOR
## Camouflage and Markings World War II

By Jim Mesko

Color By Don Greer
David Gebhardt
Darren Glenn

squadron/signal publications

**Cover:** An M4A3E2 of the 37th Tank Battalion, 4th Armored Division, C Company that led the spearhead to relieve Bastogne on 26 December 1944. "COBRA KING" claims the honor of being the first tank into Bastogne.

COPYRIGHT 2005 SQUADRON/SIGNAL PUBLICATIONS, INC.
1115 CROWLEY DRIVE CARROLLTON, TEXAS 75011-5010

All rights reserved. No part of this publication may be reproduced, stored in a retrieval system or transmitted in any form by means electrical, mechanical or otherwise, without written permission of the publisher.

**ISBN 0-89747-492-9**

If you have any photographs of aircraft, armor, soldiers or ships of any nation, particularly wartime snapshots, why not share them with us and help make Squadron/Signal's books all the more interesting and complete in the future. Any photograph sent to us will be copied and the original returned. The donor will be fully credited for any photos used. Please send them to:

Squadron/Signal Publications, Inc.
1115 Crowley Drive
Carrollton, TX 75011-5010

Если у вас есть фотографии самолетов, вооружения, солдат или кораблей любой страны, особенно, снимки времен войны, поделитесь с нами и помогите сделать новые книги издательства Эскадрон/Сигнал еще интереснее. Мы переснимем ваши фотографии и вернем оригиналы. Имена приславших снимки будут сопровождать все опубликованные фотографии. Пожалуйста, присылайте фотографии по адресу:

Squadron/Signal Publications, Inc.
1115 Crowley Drive
Carrollton, TX 75011-5010

軍用機、装甲車両、兵士、軍艦などの写真を所持しておられる方はいらっしゃいませんか？どの国のものでも結構です。作戦中に撮影されたものが特に良いのです。Squadron/Signal社の出版する刊行物において、このような写真は内容を一層充実し、興味深くすることができます。当方にお送り頂いた写真は、複写の後お返しいたします。出版物中に写真を使用した場合は、必ず提供者のお名前を明記させて頂きます。お写真は下記にご送付ください。

Squadron/Signal Publications, Inc.
1115 Crowley Drive
Carrollton, TX 75011-5010

# This book is dedicated to all U.S. armor troops

## Photo Credits

Patton Armor and Cavalry Museum
National Archives
U. S. Army
U.S. Marine Corps
Richard Hunnicutt
Mike Green

The scene at right illustrates life in the real camouflage world. These engineers from the 84th Engineer Camouflage Battalion are putting the finishing touches on an M5A1. Note how they are spraying over sandbags, cables, tarps, spare treads, and even the muddy suspension. The camouflage pattern probably is broad black bands over an Olive Drab base, although there is the possibility it could also be Earth Brown over Olive Drab. With black and white photos there is always the possibility for interpretive error with regards to color. In early 1945, black over Olive Drab was by far the more common pattern used, so this would be the most logical choice. (USA/NA)

## INTRODUCTION

While there has been a large amount of material written about the markings and camouflage of German armored and soft-skinned vehicles in World War II, little has been written concerning the similar treatment of American vehicles during the war. For the most part what has been written recently has been done by American author Steven Zaloga in a series of modeling and historical articles in several magazines, along with an earlier book on the subject. It is indeed unfortunate that American armor and vehicles have been so poorly served, since there are numerous examples of interesting and unique camouflage patterns and markings from every major theater where American vehicles saw service.

With this in mind, **U.S. Armor Camouflage and Markings World War II** attempts to give a broad overview of the various schemes and identifications used on U.S. vehicles from 1941 to 1945. Of necessity, the opening section of the book dealing with the early years prior to World War II only touches on this area so as to set the stage for the wartime subject. Anyone with an interest in the earlier time frame should consult *Organization and Markings of the United States Armored Units, 1918-1941* by Charles Lemons, curator of the Patton Cavalry and Armor Museum at Fort Knox. This is an outstanding book, and this author highly recommends it to anyone with an interest in pre-war U.S. markings.

The prevailing view of American military vehicles is that they were all Olive Drab with their markings in white. While there is a good deal of substance to this opinion, there was still a fair amount of diversity that allows the historian and modeler to find notable exceptions.

Early in the war the Army tried to establish a general pattern for markings and camouflage schemes, but because of the wide scale of deployment of units overseas, conflicting viewpoints related to these issues, a lack of adequate paint supplies, and time constraints, there was never a consensus on a uniform application of markings and camouflage. This was especially true the closer one came to the front lines, although if time and materials were available, there was often a greater uniformity. In the United States these doctrines were much more closely followed because of the fixed nature of the various installations where training took place. Yet even in something as simple as the star used as the national identification marking on all vehicles, there was a great number of variations related to its size, placement, and color, along with related markings such as the circle that was added prior to the invasion of Sicily in the summer of 1943.

Two contrasts stand out by comparison with German military markings. In the German army, paint or paste that could be diluted were supplied to AFV crews along with sprayers to help make their vehicles blend in better with the surrounding terrain. This was in addition to what rear echelon personnel had available when working on vehicles. By contrast, American equipment crews were rarely given paint or equipment, since this was considered a job for the engineer camouflage battalions. And while American aircraft, especially in the later stages of the war, were painted with extremely specific markings, this was done by ground crew at fixed installations, not by the pilots or crews themselves. In the field, tank and vehicle crews were responsible for daily maintenance of their vehicles, restocking depleted ammunition, refueling, and planning for the next day's operations, often after having spent a hard day in combat. Vehicle markings and camouflage were not high on their list of things to worry about, for obvious reasons. Of course, there were exceptions to this, especially if it might increase their chances of survival in combat. Examples of this were seen in the early days in North Africa when crews even used dried mud to break up their vehicle's silhouette in the light colored desert areas they operated in, or during the winter of 1944-1945 when the widespread use of whitewash was required to help vehicles blend in with the snowy terrain.

The result of all this is an interesting spectrum of markings and color schemes that have been overlooked for far too long. The resulting collection of photos has been selected to emphasize this diversity in markings and camouflage schemes. While the author recognizes that the majority of vehicles used by American forces did follow a general standard, there was enough divergence from this pattern to allow for an interesting and fascinating treatise.

The vast majority of the photographs included were originally taken by combat photographers of the U.S. Army and the U.S. Marine Corps. The originals now reside in the National Archives in Washington D.C. The author had the opportunity to search the Army and Marine archives prior to the photos being transferred to the National Archives. Following their transfer, additional research was done at the archives. In addition, the Patton Armor and Cavalry Museum has a large selection of photos, and their staff has been outstanding in helping the author do research there and copy photos for use in this and other Squadron/Signal books. This museum also has records and documents related to camouflage and markings. Supplementing these are various publications that deal in part with various aspects of the subject related to individual vehicles. Finally, there is a growing interest in technical manuals on U.S. vehicles from World War II, and these are available from several sources, museums, and booksellers that deal with this special area of interest. Of particular value was a reprint of AR-850-5 that dealt with markings and their placement on vehicles. In a sense the photos speak for themselves, but the captions that go with them are the responsibility of the author, and any mistakes that occur are solely his. Hopefully these will be few, but there is still a lot of uncharted ground to be covered, even this long after the end of World War II, and the author asks your indulgence in this respect.

Jim Mesko
Akron, Ohio
Summer 2005

(Above) The first American military vehicles were painted in an Olive Drab color. This was a combination of black and ochre, the actual color varying with the mixture ratio. The durability of paint from this period was not good, and it did not hold up well under the elements in the field. This Holt prime mover is being loaded onto a trailer attached to a truck with a field gun mounted on the truck bed. (USA/NA)

# WORLD WAR ONE — 1930s

The first motor vehicles acquired by the U.S. Army prior to World War I were painted in a shade of brown green which some have speculated was based on a Pullman railroad color. While no official documents have surfaced substantiating this claim, the close connection that existed between the Army and the railroads lends credence to this theory. What ever its origin, the color that eventually became standard on American military vehicles was called Olive Drab and was arrived at by simply mixing black with ochre, created a muddy olive brown shade.

By the time the U.S. entered World War I, tanks had made their appearance on the battlefield. Unfortunately there were no tanks then available for American troops except those that could be provided by the French and British. Construction plans were sent from both allies so that these designs could be manufactured in this country, but none would ever be produced in time for service in Europe during the war. Instead the French and British proved the American Expeditionary Corps with enough tanks for it to eventually field its own armored force. The majority of the FT-17 and FT-18 light tanks provided by the French were painted in three- and four-color camouflage patterns, while the British Mk IV and Mk V heavy tanks were painted in British green. The light tanks carried a spade, heart, or diamond card symbol inside a square, circle, or diamond to indicate platoon and company. The heavy tanks carried red and white stripes on the forward and rear casemates and the front of the hulls on either side.

Wartime experience with camouflage led to two opposing views among Army officers. One faction held that the natural dirt and grime of the battlefield quickly covered up any camouflage pattern and rendered it useless, while the other felt that camouflage was effective, particularly when combined with foliage and artificial means of camouflage such as netting, especially when the vehicle was dug in. These two divergent views were never resolved and provided a basis for further discussion after the war.

Following World War I the fledging American Armor Corps was dissolved and its vehicles were assigned to the infantry and cavalry. In the post-war Army it was decided to paint all combat vehicles in lusterless (flat) Olive Drab while administrative vehicles would be painted in glossy Olive Drab, and to this end the Army issued its requirements for an Olive Drab paint that was darker than the color used during the war.

The use of both flat and gloss Olive Drab caused problems. Combat vehicles actually looked lighter than administrative vehicles as the glossy finish of the latter gave them the appearance of being darker. Another problem that occurred was that the flat finish did not wear well under field conditions, resulting in a worn, scruffy look that did not sit well with the "spit and polish" attitude of the peacetime Army. As a result many units took to painting their combat vehicles in the glossy color or used spar varnish, oil, or polish to "spruce up" their vehicles. In addition, any touchup painting did not blend well due to the drying time of the paint and its inability to exactly match untouched areas of older paint. The only real solution would have been to literally paint the entire vehicle, something that was not feasible. Eventually, in the mid-1930s, the Army had a more durable enamel paint developed that had a quicker drying time and a more glossy finish. This was to be used in peacetime, while the flat Olive Drab would be used in time of war.

(Below) With the entry of the U.S. into World War I, American camouflage was influenced by both the French multi-colored schemes and British solid bronze green. This light truck has received a multi-color scheme, even down to the canvas cover over the cargo compartment. The colors were believed to be green, brown, and yellow with black outlines. (USA/NA)

# MARKINGS

The Tank Corps was abolished in 1920 and its tanks distributed between the infantry and cavalry. Prior to that some tanks had been marked with the Tank Corps insignia, a trisected triangle in yellow (top),

(Above) The majority of the tanks employed by the American Expeditionary Force (A.E.F.) in France were French built FT-17s. Many of these were in the French three– and four–tone camouflage scheme. (Buschay via Squadron Signal)

(Above) The Army developed a multi-colored scheme of its own based on the French patterns. This was composed of green, brown, yellow, tan, and white with a black outline, as seen on this FT-17 light tank. (USA/PAM)

red (right), and blue (left). Traces of this marking could be seen on tanks taken out of storage in years to come.

The subject of vehicle markings was dealt with in Army Regulation AR-850-5, which was overseen by the Adjutant General's office. One of the more common markings to be seen in the post-World War I years was the branch of service insignia — crossed sabers for the cavalry and crossed rifles for the infantry. The unit number was placed above the sabers or rifles while below them was the company designation. Another type of identification consisted of the unit's designation and vehicle number written in a single line of alphanumeric characters, but this was not as common as the service insignia. Both types often had the unit crest applied in front of the markings as an additional aid to identification.

Other markings were sometimes used to identify a particular vehicle. A good example of this practice can be seen in the photo of the T-3 Christie tank in the photograph on page 6. Normally these markings were carried on the front of the tank.

Tanks were spread out between the infantry and cavalry and further divided up between Army and National Guard units. Variations were quite common since AR-850-5 only laid down general guidelines, thus allowing for each unit's interpretation of the instructions. As a result there were a variety of markings that evolved during the 1930s. Some of these were quite colorful. Cavalry units used the red and white command guidon painted on the side of combat car turrets with letters and numbers in it to identify the unit. Some regimental commanders used a plain white guidon as a backdrop for the regimental crest. Other units used the unit crest on their turrets as a means of identification. While all of these were colorful and helped identify the units, they would have been very impractical in time of war. And with war clouds gathering in Europe in the late 1930s the Army began to look at more subtle markings to increase security and make identification by any potential enemy more difficult.

(Below) This T5 prime mover has a nice glossy appearance for a parade or display after being cleaned up. It is from the 68th Field Artillery, Battery "B," as can be seen by the crossed cannons on the door with the unit designation on the top and the battery underneath. (USA/PAM)

(Above) Following World War I the U.S. Army went back to Olive Drab as its basic color. For administrative vehicles it was gloss, while tactical vehicles were in flat or lusterless Olive Drab. The flat Olive Drab weathered badly, and vehicles often were given a coat of spar varnish or wax to give them a more spit-and-polished look in the peacetime Army. This M1 armored car from the 1st Cavalry, Troop "A," has a dull appearance from its flat finish and light coating of dust. When back at its base, Fort Knox, it undoubtedly would be cleaned up to a shiny finish until the next field maneuvers. (USA/NA)

(Below) During summer maneuvers at New York's Pine Camp these three Christie T3s sit alongside the road during a lull in the movement. Each is labeled with the tank's designation and tactical number on the bow, its name on both sides of the driver's compartment, and the crossed rifles of the infantry with the unit and company designation above and below the rifles, as well as the regimental crest. In spite of their being out in the field on maneuvers, these vehicles are surprisingly clean. (USA/NA)

# GATHERING STORM CLOUDS

With war clouds gathering in Europe due to the rise of Adolph Hitler, the U.S. Army began to look at its state of training, preparedness, and equipment. The use of tanks in Poland stunned the world and added a new word to the vocabulary of warfare: *blitzkrieg*. This led in the summer of 1940 to the formation of the Armored Force and the activation of National Guard tank units into independent tank battalions. As these battalions formed up a wide variety of markings were evident. Uniformity was lacking, as each unit tended to develop its own markings. These ranged from the actual spelling out of the unit's name to the use of geometric shapes and card symbols as had been used in World War I.

The five armored divisions seem to have had a more planned markings arrangement. At first a system similar to that used by the infantry, consisting of geometric shapes and colors, was used by the 1st and 2nd Armored Divisions. Gradually they shifted to colored bands around the turret for their regiments. Letters designating the company and the tactical number also began to appear on the turrets. This type of marking also was adopted by the 3rd Armored Division. The 3rd began placing a small miniature Armored Forces Triangle between the company letter and number on the turret and also at several positions on tank hulls. The 4th Armored Division followed none of these patterns, instead using either an open triangle or square with the company letter in it. Specific colors were used for each regiment. Information is lacking on the markings used by the 5th Armored Division.

This period was one of constant change as units were moved around and equipment exchanged. From this experimentation would be developed a system of markings that would satisfy both the needs for identification and security of the new American armored force.

**This M1 combat car from the 1st Cavalry carries the unit crest on the turret. Armed only with machine guns, the M1 was the precursor to the M3 series. Although inadequate, such vehicles at least allowed some semblance of training in mobile warfare. (USA/PAM)**

**The large white command guidon containing the unit crest shown on this M1 was part of the peacetime army's colorful marking system. Such markings did not last long once war actually broke out. (USA/PAM)**

(Above) A good part of the mechanized might of the U.S. Army is visible here during maneuvers in 1939 by the 1st Army. A variety of M1 combat cars and M3 scout cars are visible in the photo, all marked with the unit crest of the 13th Cavalry. Much was learned during these maneuvers relating to command and control, logistics, and planning, which later proved useful with the formation of armored divisions. (USA/NA)

(Left) Not particularly conducive to keeping the unit's identity a secret were the markings on this M2A3 light tank from the 2nd Tank Company. The crest on the sponson and the lower hull are the platoon markings, while the 2nd Division's Indian head insignia is just in front of the company designation. As war approached it was obvious that new markings were going to be needed. (USA/NA)

(Below) These M2A2 light tanks of Company "D," 192nd Tank Battalion, carry a green spade outlined in orange for 3rd Army maneuvers in 1941. This unit was eventually sent to the Philippines in late 1941; it and the 194th Tank Battalion were the first American armored units to see ground combat in World War II. (USA/NA )

(Above) This M2A2 from Company "B," 68th Infantry, formed part of a provisional tank brigade in 1939 at Fort Knox. The events in Europe helped the Army high command break out of its traditional approach to tank employment and eventually led to the formation of several armored divisions patterned after those used by Germany in France during 1940. Geometric markings were often used for different companies as part of an ongoing attempt to find an effective and secure way of identification in the field. (USA/NA)

(Right) A column of M2A2s and M2A3s sits on the side of the road during maneuvers in 1939. At least three different geometric shapes can be seen on the front of the sponsons. The red "C" indicated the company commander's tank, and the various numbers are the individual tank's number. The triangle is yellow with a red outline. The unit is the 66th Infantry Regiment. (USA/NA)

(Below) An M2 Medium tank of the 3rd Platoon, Company "F," 67th Infantry Regiment, during spring maneuvers in 1940. The disk on the side is in yellow, while the outline and the number are in red. Both the 66th and 67th Tank Battalions used similar markings. (USA/PAM)

(Above) This T12 with bits of foliage for camouflage takes part in war games in the autumn of 1941. The cloth tied around the engine signified either the red or blue forces during the games. The initial batch of T12s eventually were shipped in late 1941 to the Philippines to support the 192nd and 194th Tank Battalions in the forlorn defense of the islands. (USA/NA)

(Left) An M1 combat car from the 1st Cavalry Regiment moves along a stream at Ft. Knox in 1939. The "2" on the front hull faces forward for recognition from aircraft approaching from the rear. Note how the driver's hatch has had the white portion of the "2" that is covered when the hatch is open painted on the inside so that the number would still be visible from the air. The use of a name on the forward part of the sponson was unusual at this time. (USA/NA)

(Below) The attack on Pearl Harbor added a new sense of urgency to training the armored forces. These M3s take part in an exercise in the California Desert with A-20 light bombers. Due to a shortage of medium tanks, they carry a white "M" on their turrets to indicate their role as medium tanks. Barely discernable around the turrets is a yellow band. (USA/NA)

# NATIONAL MARKINGS AND STARS

There was little in the way of prominent national identification on early American tanks and vehicles. Some tank crews painted the Tank Corps emblem on their vehicles, but when the Corps was dissolved these markings were painted over in most cases. In the early 1920s the 2nd Tank Company assigned to the 2nd Infantry Division painted rough stars on the turrets of their M1917 light tanks.

With the amalgamation of infantry and cavalry tanks into the Armored Force as war drew near in the 1940s, the Armored Force's triangle began to appear on some tanks. This triangle of blue, red, and yellow was used on tanks of the 1st Armored Division with the unit's number placed in the yellow portion and a tracked insignia underneath it. The triangle was located on the front of the hull.

The 2nd Armored Division adopted an experimental aerial recognition insignia during April and May of 1941. This consisted of a white star inside a red circle with a blue circle in the center of the star. This was identical to the markings then in use by the Army Air Corps but with the red and blue reversed. This marking was carried on the hull front and sides and the tops and sides of the turrets. On wheeled vehicles these markings were carried on the front and back.

When the 3rd Armored Division was organized in the spring of 1941 it received some tanks from the 2nd Armored Division with the circle and star insignia. In addition, the 3rd also marked its tanks with small four-inch Armored Force triangles. These could be on both front fenders or the final drive, in the rear, either above the fenders or on them, and between the identification letter and number on the turret. Variations of this scheme occurred, but these markings were only carried for a short period.

Following the attack on Pearl Harbor in December 1941, a more concerted effort was made to bring about some form of standardization of markings. A yellow star was selected by Armored Forces Headquarters as the national insignia for use on armored vehicles. Eventually the Army adopted a white star as the national insignia for all vehicles in one of its early AR-850-5 editions. While the Armored Force continued to use the yellow star in some cases, notably the 1st Armored Division in North Africa, the general availability of white paint coupled with less access to yellow paint resulted in many tanks and vehicles being marked with white stars.

An interesting variation occurred with the white star on a few vehicles in North Africa. On some sand-colored vehicles the star was placed in a blue circle since the star tended to blend in with the light colored background. This was a rare marking, since few American vehicles were painted in overall sand.

Following the North African campaign, Armored Forces Headquarters ordered that a circle be placed around the star to aid in long-range identification. This change resulted from the star's appearing at long range to look like the crosses used on German vehicles. The circles eventually appeared in two forms, a continuous circle and a segmented circle. The reason for the segmented circle was quite simple. When stencils were placed on the vehicles, only the portion that was cut out was painted in. The unpainted portion remained when the stencil was removed, resulting in a segmented circle.

During the invasion of Sicily, Operation HUSKY, orders were issued to paint the circles yellow. Orders were also issued to make the circle at least double the width of the current circles. This led to some very unusual star and circle patterns with some circles being grossly out of proportion to the stars they encircled. There were numerous variations of these patterns seen during the Sicily operation, and many of these later carried over into the Italian campaign.

As American forces prepared for the invasion of France in the spring of 1944, a vast array of AFVs and other vehicles were readied for the invasion. All of these carried some sort of star for recognition, and a circle around the star was also widely used. However, there was a vast amount of variation as to size, placement, and composition of the star with and without the circle. The circle and star also became a recognized marking for aerial identification on Allied vehicles, which often carried it atop turrets, engine decks, and hoods to forestall attacks by Allied fighter bombers.

After the initial landings the Allies became bogged down in the Normandy beachhead. The close-in nature of the fighting led to a variety of camouflage to help conceal the various vehicles. The large white stars were often felt to serve as aiming points for German gunners. This resulted in many crews covering them over with mud or thick grease or painting them out. Again, there was wide variation in this, even within individual units. The result was a range of combinations that followed no official pattern or program. Also, as tankers became aware of the limited protection their armor provided against German tanks, anti-tank guns, and panzerfausts, supplemental armor protection became common. This took the form of sandbags, logs, concrete, track links, and extra armor plate. Often these covered the stars, and nothing was done to repaint them if the surface lent itself to that. It was not unusual to see tanks and other AFVs completely devoid of any stars on their hull and turret sides as the war progressed.

Markings atop the turret and engine deck were left for aerial identification purposes, but those on the engine decks were often covered with extra gear. Thus by the end of the war there was little in the way of any systematic set of star markings except those that appeared on newly issued equipment.

During 1941 the 1st Armored Division used the Armor Forces three colored triangle with the number "1" placed in the upper yellow section above the track links in the center of the triangle. This M2A1 medium tank, from the 69th Armored Regiment, Company B, moves down a road followed by an M2 halftrack. The cloth tied around the turret is red while there is probably a broken blue line around the base of the turret. The Armored Forces triangle can be seen just underneath the B-4 on the front glacis plate. (USA/PAM)

(Above) The 2nd and 3rd Armored Divisions tried another type of marking, using a variation of the Army Air Corps star and circle. However, instead of a blue outer circle and red center dot, these colors were reversed. This 3rd Army M3 crosses a pontoon bridge during maneuvers in mid-December 1941. The two lead vehicles have their front stars pointing down while the two rear vehicles have their stars pointing upward. They also have the markings on the side and on the rear of the turrets. Some vehicles also had them painted on the tops of the turret. (USA/PAM)

(Above) On this light M2A4 the insignia was painted on the post separating the two drivers' hatches and overlapped onto them. On light tanks the insignia was not carried on the sides but on the rear of the turret and on top of the turret next to the cupola. This tank is from the 68th Armored Regiment, Company F. Turret markings are in white. (USA/ NA)

(Below) In January 1942 a yellow star was adopted as the identification markings for all armor vehicles. In the summer of 1942 the yellow color was changed to white. This took time to implement, and the use of yellow stars went on for a time after the changeover to white. These M3 light tanks at the Desert Training Center in California display the yellow stars on the sides of their turrets along with a yellow band around the turret. The "M" is to indicate that the tanks are playing the role of medium tanks due to the shortage of vehicles at the time. (USA/NA)

(Below) From the tone of the white paint on the turret interior it appears that the stars and bands on these M2 light and M3 medium tanks are in white. Note how some of the hatches of the M2s have stars on their inside covers for aerial identification. Of interest is how some of these stars face forward while others face toward the rear of the vehicles. (USA/NA)

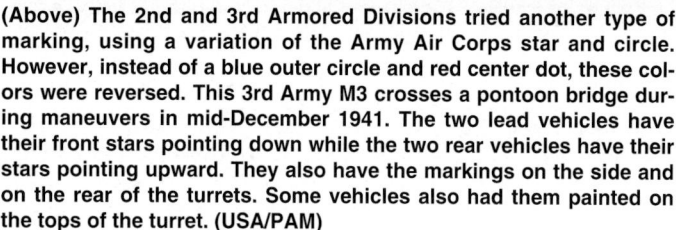

(Above and Above Right) While guidelines were given for both the star's placement and size, there were variations since the stars were often applied either by field units or depots. This led to variations even at the same installations, as exhibited by these M2 halftrack models with different size stars on their engine hoods. (USA/PAM)

(Right) This destroyed M2 in North Africa shows how differences occurred in the shape of the star when rough cut stencils or tape was used. This yellow star is not as precise as those normally applied to vehicles. (USA/NA)

(Below) During the invasion of North Africa, American tanks were painted with oversized stars in the hopes that French forces would not fire on the invading U.S. troops. In addition, American flags were displayed on the hull sides. These M5s are part of a post-invasion parade reviewed in Morocco by President Roosevelt in January 1943. Note the variations in the placement of the flags on the hull sides. The stars are yellow as ascertained by comparing their tone with the white of the stripes on the flags. (USA/NA)

(Left) A relatively rare marking in North Africa was the star on a blue circle like that used on aircraft. This M2 halftrack fitted with a 37mm anti-tank gun from an M6 truck carries this marking on the side and rear. The yellow square with the red "Y" on the side signifies the 601st Tank Destroyer Battalion. (USA/PAM)

(Below) For the invasion of Sicily it was decided to paint a circle around the star to help with long-range and aerial identification. Sometimes this could lead to interesting combinations as on this M7 with a large star on its side. The circle was adapted to fit the star, resulting in the uncompleted lower portion. (USA/NA)

(Below) Markings were sometimes applied without benefit of stencils, resulting in the rough application shown here. Both the star and circle on this M4 were obviously hand-painted. The crew has liberated a beach umbrella to help protect them from the elements. (USA/NA)

Often the stencils had tape holding them on the vehicle's surface, and when the stencils were removed a gap was left, creating a segmented appearance if the areas were not filled in as seen on this M12 self-propelled gun. This was a very common occurrence and not another type of official marking. (USA/NA)

(Below) During the Sicily invasion the circle was sometimes painted in yellow as seen on the sides and fronts of these M7 "Priests" Notice the different sizes and breaks in the circle, especially on the closest vehicle, which highlights how the variation could exist. The closest M7 also appears to have the lower hull painted in a lighter color as a counter-shading attempt at camouflage, a relatively rare pattern used in the Italian Theater. (USA/NA)

(Below) Another interesting star and circle variation was the use of circles as wide or wider than the star with a small star inside the circle. This M5 carries such a combination on its side and exhibits the breaks in the stencil by the tape. (USA/NA)

(Above) Another M5 shows the oversized circle with star inside on the hull and turret top. The star appears to be the half the diameter of the circle. (USA/NA)

(Below) If two stars are better, then three is best. This M18 "Hellcat" carries three stars due to its torsion bar suspension, which was more common on German AFVs than on American. M18s carried these more visible markings to cut down on misidentifications. (USA/NA)

(Above) If one star is good, then two are better! This probably occurred when the extra bogie wheel covered the original star and the crew added another one. Either due to lack of paint or time they left the original star. The unit codes have been painted on the machine gun pulpit, a common practice on the M7. (USA/NA)

(Below) Unfortunately the stars also provided a good aiming point for German tankers and anti-tank crews. This is graphically illustrated by the two holes through the stars on the side of this M4 being recovered by an M26 "Dragon Wagon." (USA/NA)

(Above) To reduce the star's visibility to German gunners, a number of things were tried. The crew of this M7 has toned down the star by covering it with mud. The circle may have been added after this was done and can be seen to have been crudely painted on the side of this M7, even with the help of a stencil. (USA/NA)

(Left) This M7 crew has also used mud, but in this case they have covered both the star and circle with it. This M7 had the star in white while the circle was in yellow. The star and circle on the three-piece glacis has also been covered with mud. The vehicle is dug in at the Anzio beachhead. (USA/NA)

(Below) This M7 has had the star and circle overpainted in a dark color, possibly black, but it could also be blue or red, as they have similar tonal values in a black-and-white photo. A small cartoon on a panel is just visible forward of the star.

# SERIAL, UNIT, AND CLASSIFICATION MARKINGS

## Registration Numbers

In the Army, every vehicle had a registration number for identification purposes. This War Department (W.D.) number was kept by the Quartermaster General until 1942, when the responsibility was transferred to the Ordnance Department. The registration number was painted on a prominent point on the vehicle. For jeeps, trucks, halftracks, and other wheeled vehicles, this was usually the side of the engine compartment. On tanks and other AFVs this was usually toward the rear. Normally the legend "U.S.A." was painted above the registration number or in front of it. Prior to 1942 the letter "W" for War Department was painted in front of the serial number, but this practice was stopped that year. Some vehicles had the letter "S" at the end of the registration number. This signified that the vehicle had been modified to suppress radio interference by its electrical system over a frequency range of 0.5 to 30 megacycles.

The registration number also served as a means to identify the class of vehicle from either the first or first two digits of the number. Below is the breakdown of the numbers.

0: Trailers and semi-trailers, wheeled and motor drawn, excluding kitchen trailers
1: Passenger cars, both open and closed
2: Trucks, light delivery, panel, pick-up, utility, and weapons carriers
3: Light trucks, cargo, dump, and tractor
4: Medium trucks, cargo, dump, and tractor
5: Heavy trucks, cargo, dump, tractor, and tank transporter
6: Motorcycle, both single and with sidecars, and motor scooters
7: Ambulances, field and metropolitan/city
8: Tractors, wheeled, light, medium, and heavy
9: Track-laying tractors, light, medium, and heavy
00: Maintenance trucks, light repair, small arms, repair and wrecking
10: Kitchen trailers, motor drawn
20: Reconnaissance trucks, jeeps, buses, and carry-alls
30: Tanks, light, medium, heavy and some special tank-based vehicles
40: Track-laying vehicles, including cargo carriers, halftracks, motor gun carriages and non-combat types
50: Fire trucks, fire and crash vehicles
60: Special and technical vehicles including armored cars, generator, office, radio, searchlight, sterilizing, and water purification
80: Tank and sprinkler trucks including tank trucks and light and heavy refueling trucks

### These were grouped in the following categories
A) General Service – 1, 2, 3, 4, 5, 6, 8, 20
B) General and Special Service – 0
C) Special Service – 7, 9, 00, 10, 50, 60, 80
D) Combat – 30, 40

For security purposes there was no discernable pattern when blocks of numbers were assigned to type. This made it impossible for the enemy to determine the number of tanks or vehicles manufactured based on registration numbers on captured ones. Five or six digit registration numbers were common up to 1942, but then larger numbers became the norm as American industry kicked into high gear.

## Bumper Codes

In August 1942 AR-850-5 included a comprehensive set of bumper codes to replace those currently in use. These new codes were broken down into three groups of letters. The first group dealt with major corps, divisions, and centers. The second group contained regiments, brigades, and separate battalions. The third group included companies and other small units. Normal procedure was for the first and second groups to be painted on the right side of the bumper or hull while the third group would appear on the left side. The letters used for each group are shown below.

### First Group

| | |
|---|---|
| Infantry division | Arabic numeral |
| Armored Division | Arabic numeral followed by triangle 3 inches high with 1/4-inch stroke |
| Cavalry Division | Arabic number followed by letter "C" |
| Army Corps | Roman numeral |
| Cavalry Corps | Roman numeral followed by letter "C" |
| Armored Corps | Roman numeral followed by triangle 3 inches high |
| Army | Arabic numeral followed by letter "A" |
| Air Force | Arabic numeral followed by star 3 inches high |
| Zone of Communication | ZC |
| Army Ground Forces | AGF |
| Service of Supplies | SOS |
| General Headquarters | GHQ |
| Zone of Interior | ZI |
| Reception Center | RC |
| Replacement Training Center | RTC preceded by arm or service symbol |
| Training Center | TC preceded by arm or service symbol |
| Firing Center | FC preceded by arm or service symbol |
| All others | Non-conflicting letters |

### Second Group

| | |
|---|---|
| Airborne | AB |
| Army Air Force Units | Star 3 inches high |
| Antiaircraft | AA |
| Amphibious | AM |
| Cavalry | C |
| Chemical Warfare Service | G |
| Coastal Artillery Corps | CA |
| Corps of Engineers | E |
| Field Artillery Infantry | F or FA |
| Infantry | I preceded by dash 1/2 inch square |
| Medical Department | M |
| Military Police | P |
| Ordnance Department | O preceded by dash 1/2 inch square |
| Quartermaster Corps | Q |
| Signal Corps | S |
| Tank Destroyer | TD |
| Tank Group | TG |

### Third group

| | |
|---|---|
| Headquarters | HQ |
| Service Company | SV |
| Headquarters not previously identified | Numerical designation of battalion followed by letters "HQ" |
| Service Company not previously identified | Battalion number followed by letters "SV" |
| Lettered Company | Letter designation |
| Separate Company identified in second group | X or abbreviation of company |
| Antitank | AT |
| Maintenance | MT |
| Heavy Weapons | HW |
| Cannon | CN |
| Reconnaissance | R |
| Train | TN |
| Weapons | W |
| Name Company | Non-conflicting letters preceded by battalion |

The placement of these codes on bumpers and tank hulls followed the general pattern indicated earlier, but there were also exceptions to the practice. Some M7 self-propelled gun units painted their codes on the side of the machine gun enclosure or "pulpit" for better visibility since the hulls tended to get covered with mud. Also, the use of supplemental armor as the war progressed made it difficult to place the codes on the front of tanks, and often tanks were left unmarked on the front.

The 14th Armored Division often painted codes on their tanks' gun tubes when the hull was obscured by supplemental sandbag armor. From photographs it appears that this division was the only one that practiced this procedure. Other variations did occur, but the general practice of bumper placement was followed by most units.

**Unit Markings**

Unlike the British, German, French, and even Italian armored units, there was little if any standardization of unit markings among the main armored divisions of the U. S. Army during World War II. Within certain divisions there were general practices that were followed, but aside from the bumper codes, divisions developed their own and often unique set of markings. The units that did so are listed below in numerical order.

**1st Armored Division**: This division used a series of slanted bars to indicate the company, the slant of the bars indicating the battalion. For the 1st Armored Regiment a circle next to the bar indicated the company. For the 13th Armored Regiment a square was used for the company. These were usually painted in yellow. Headquarters companies used a triangle in the latter stages of the campaign. Often a small number was used to denote to which platoon the tank belonged. Some platoons eventually added slash lines to one of the arms of the star to indicate the platoon. A platoon number was sometimes added in the star also.

When the unit landed in Italy a series of colored bands on the gun barrels and turret bars was used to indicate the company and battalion. Except in the case of a white background the bands and bars were outlined in white. Command tanks often had either a white circle or an outline around their bars.

**2nd Armored Division**: This division used a set of markings similar to the 1st Armored Division, but used a narrow horizontal bar in place of the wider one from their sister unit.

The 66th Armored Regiment used a series of squares on this bar to indicate the company.

The 67th Armored Regiment used a "T" to indicate the company.

The unit was transferred to England for Operation OVERLORD, the invasion of France. During the fighting in Normandy the unit painted large tactical numbers and letters in yellow on the sides of their tanks and other AFVs. These indicated the company and individual number within the company. Many vehicles also carried names that began with the letter of the company. On medium tanks this name was normally on the side of the turret. On light tanks, halftracks, and armored cars the name was painted on the hull sides and on halftracks also on the rear. These prominent markings were gradually painted over when they were found to provide good aiming points for German tanks and anti-tank guns. The 2nd also began to paint their vehicles with bands of black paint to help camouflage them during this period.

**3rd Armored Division**: Like the 2nd Armored division, this division also began to paint prominent tactical numbers and letters on their vehicles, along with names beginning with the company letter. The 3rd Armored Division also began to camouflage their tanks and AFVs with bands of black. As with the 2nd Armored Division, the stars and large numbers were gradually painted out as being too conspicuous.

**6th Armored Division**: This division used a series of geometric designs for a short period of time. These also proved to be too prominent and were removed. By late 1944 their tanks were carrying large numbers on the sides of their hulls.

**11th Armored Division**: This Division used markings on their stars similar to those used in North Africa by the 1st Armored Division. The number of slashes indicated the company while the position on the arm

(Above) This M5A1 carries the standard markings prior to specific unit and divisional markings being added. National stars are painted on the front and hull sides. Next to the front star is the bridging classification consisting of a yellow circle with a number denoting the weight in tons of a fully loaded vehicle. A nickname is on the side of the hull, though not related to a specific company as might be carried in the field. Behind it is a listing of the vehicle's basic dimensions and specifications. At the very back is the vehicle's serial number, beginning with "30" which indicates a tank. Temporary markings are chalked onto the front fenders. (USA/NA)

of the the star denoted the battalion.

**12th Armored Division**: A series of chevrons and bars on the side of the hull was used to indicate companies and battalions. Small circles atop these indicated the platoon.

**14th Armored Division**: The main identification point for tanks of this Division were the bumper codes on the gun barrels of their M4 tanks. This was due to the addition of supplemental sandbag armor that made it difficult to place these codes in their normal position on the transmission housing.

(Below) A variation of the bridging circle is this example with split numbers. These indicate the vehicle's weight with and without an ammunition trailer. (USA/NA)

(Above) The Army developed a registration number system for its vehicles that was relatively easy to decipher, using the first number or number and "0" for identification. Motorcycles began with "6" while "20" was for reconnaissance trucks, jeeps, carryalls, and buses. The legend "USA" either preceded the number or was above it as seen on these two vehicles from what appears to be the 1st battalion of an artillery unit. (USA/PAM)

## Miscellaneous Markings

American vehicles carried other markings and identification lettering that helped denote a variety of things. Often rough letters and numbers were chalked on hulls and bodies for shipping purposes. These might include the destination, ship assigned to, and loading order or placement. The use of chalk made it easy to wipe these off once they had served their purpose.

Other more formal markings might include information of a specific nature, such as weight, dimensions, and instructions related to vehicle maintenance. These were usually kept on the vehicle until it got into combat, at which time they were either overpainted or wore off.

(Below) Light trucks such as pick-ups, utility trucks, delivery trucks, and weapons carriers had registration numbers beginning with "2." The "W" preceding the number, the use of which began in 1926, indicated the War Department. (USA/PAM)

(Above) Tank serial numbers began with "30" as seen on this M2 medium tank during maneuvers in 1940. The markings are in white making them easy to see, a concern both for concealment and security. (USA/NA)

(Below) Experiments were conducted with a number of colors to find one that was better suited for reduced visibility. These included Black and Dark Earth, but eventually Blue Drab was selected due to its ability to blend in tonally with the Olive Drab base coat. Even under close scrutiny the markings on the rear of these M3 Lees is almost impossible to see at a distance. Unfortunately this is of little value due to the highly visible white company markings and colorful star insignia similar to that used for a time by the Air Corps, but with the blue and red reversed. (USA/NA)

(Above) Registration numbers beginning with "40" were used to identify a variety of tracked vehicles, primarily combat types. These included halftracks such as this M3A1, which had large registration numbers on its engine compartment in white. A careful look just under the 315 at the end shows the remnants of the original number in yellow. The "S" at the end of the serial number indicates that the vehicle has been radio-suppressed. (USA/PAM)

(Above) Other vehicles in the "40" category included both light and heavy self-propelled artillery, usually based on tank chassis. This M8 HMC of the 15th Cavalry, 94th Infantry Division, awaits orders to open fire near Lorient, Belgium in late 1944. It carries a name on the hull side and features both the regular star and star in a circle. (USA/NA)

(Below) This M12 is an example of the "40" serial on a heavy self-propelled mount. The name "BUCCANEER" on the side would indicate it belonged to "B" battery, as it was the practice of such units to name each vehicle in the battery with a name starting with the battery letter. (USA/NA)

(Below) Tank destroyers were also included in this grouping. Normally on tanks and similar vehicles the numbers were toward the rear, often with the "U.S.A." legend above the number. This M18 also has a pinup painted on the side and a bridging classification number in a yellow circle on the front of the hull. (USA/NA)

(Above) The "60" group originally included specialty and technical vehicles and was expanded to include armored cars. This M8 has its numbers above the storage rack along with the "S" added at the end. This was a more common placement of the number. (USA/NA)

(Below) The "9" serial range included track laying tractors and fully tracked amphibious vehicles. This M4 high speed tractor has its serial along with a star on the rear panel of the ammunition bay. Bumper markings indicate it is vehicle number 16 from the 999th Field Artillery, Battery C. All markings are in white. (USA/PAM)

(Above) On M10s and M36s the serial numbers were often painted further forward due to the racks on the sides for the extra grousers often carried toward the rear. These took up a great deal of space and made it difficult for numbers to be painted toward the rear of the vehicle. (USA/NA)

(Below) Heavy duty trucks and tank transporters were in the "5" serial range. An M26 armored recovery tractor pulls a "PANTHER" through Geilenkirchen, December, 1944. Just above the serial number is a pin-up. The bumper carries the codes "9A" for 9th Armored on the right and 464th Ordnance Company on the left. The white outline may have been a personal touch by the crew or used as reference for night work. Two stars are carried on the large front plate of the vehicle, not a common practice on such vehicles. (USA/PAM)

(Above) This LVT-4 carries its serial number on the rear ramp in oversized numbers and letters. LVTs were used in Europe only toward the end of the war, and markings varied widely on them. (USA/PAM)

(Below) The utility version of the M8, the M20, was also included in the "60" serial group. This vehicle has been modified as a command vehicle for General George Patton, the ring mount over the open compartment having been replaced by a pedestal mount. The serial markings have been split with the "U.S.A." legend on top and the number below it. This was less common than layouts seen on the previous M8. (USA/PAM)

(Above) By comparison with the above LVT-4, this LVT-2 has a much smaller serial number in black on the lower right side of the rear plate. Other differences are the lack of a side star, a larger rear star, and a total lack of tactical markings aside from the chalked-on number on the left. (USA/NA)

(Below) This M3A1 carries very simple markings during training in late 1942. It is from the 37th Armored Regiment, Company H, and is the 15th vehicle in the unit. There are no markings to indicate its parent unit, the 4th Armored Division. New guidelines under AR-850-5 would add additional information and geometric symbols to indicate even more information. (USA/ Hunnicutt)

(Above) AR-850-5 laid out a fairly detailed pattern for bumper markings and where they were to be located. This M5A1 belongs to the 1st Armored Division, Combat Command A, and is vehicle 23 in the headquarters unit. Note also how the original large white star has been overpainted and replaced with a smaller star and segmented circle. (USA/NA)

(Below) Markings were normally divided with the division starting on the left when viewed from head on, then the regiment, and on the right the company. This M4 is from the 6th Armored Division, 68th Armored Regiment, Company A, and is vehicle 36. To help prevent air attack by Allied aircraft a large tarp with a star and circle and an colored identification panel are carried atop the engine deck. (USA/NA)

(Above) This M3A1 shows the new type of detail carried under the revisions set forth by AR-850-5. The triangle indicated both an armored division and regiment. Thus, this tank was from the 7th Armored Division, 31st Armored Regiment, Company D. The number "1" indicated it was the first vehicle in the company. Markings could either be in white or yellow. (USA/Hunnicutt)

(Below) While it was the normal practice to have the markings in a single line, sometimes this was not possible as in the case of the three-piece transmission cover on the early M4s. It appears that this M4 was assigned to the Headquarters of the 59th Field Artillery Battalion, 5th Army. (USA/NA)

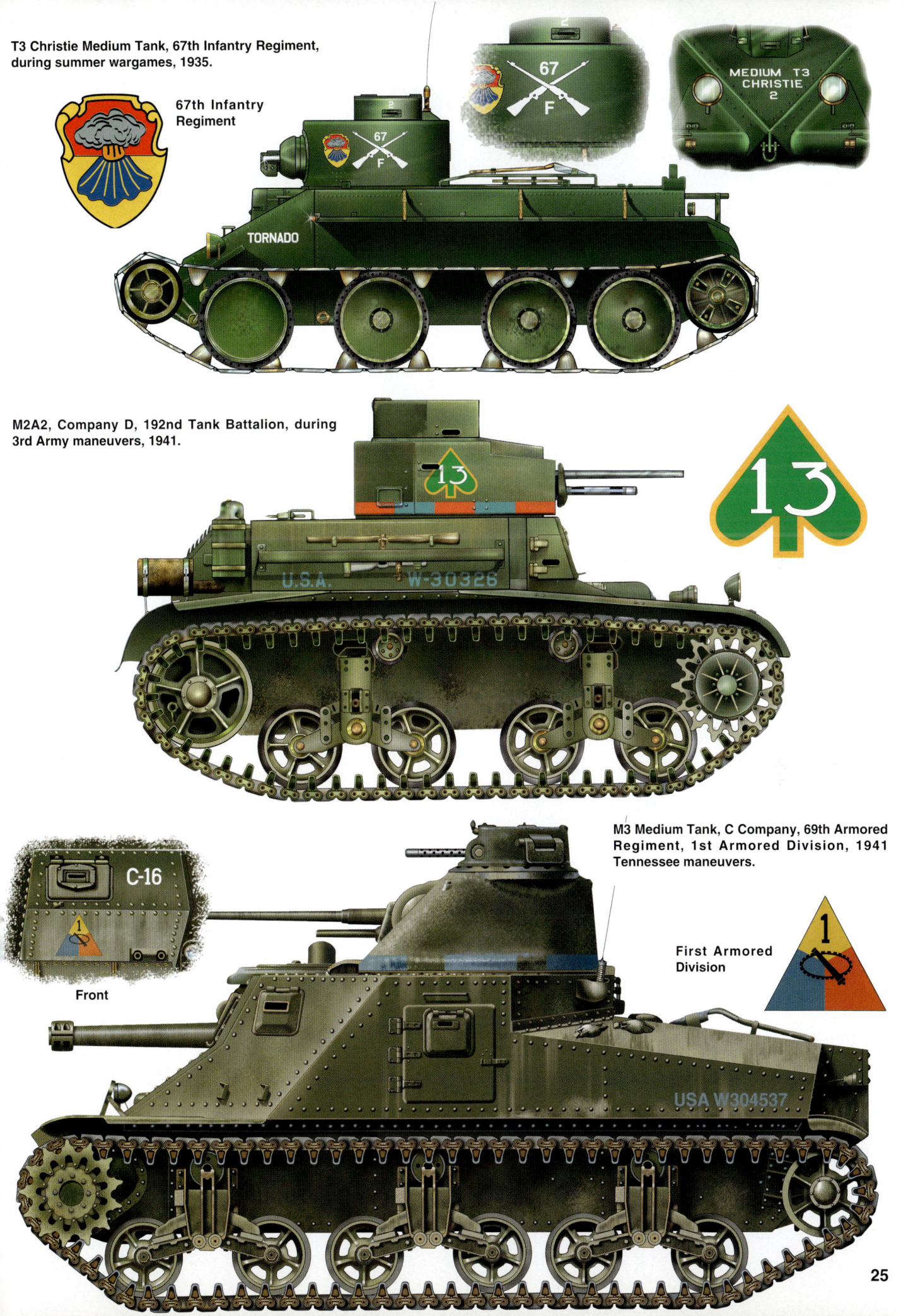

T3 Christie Medium Tank, 67th Infantry Regiment, during summer wargames, 1935.

67th Infantry Regiment

M2A2, Company D, 192nd Tank Battalion, during 3rd Army maneuvers, 1941.

M3 Medium Tank, C Company, 69th Armored Regiment, 1st Armored Division, 1941 Tennessee maneuvers.

Front

First Armored Division

(Above) Some M7 units placed their markings on the side of the machine gun pulpit in order for them to be more easily seen, as the transmission cover often became covered in mud. This late model M7 is from the 3rd Armored Division, 276th Field Artillery Regiment, Company C, and is vehicle number 7. Markings on the rear followed the normal pattern. (USA/NA)

(Below) For non-division units the largest command started on the left and worked its way down. This M18 tank destroyer is attached to the 3rd Army, 704th Tank Destroyer Battalion, Company A, and is vehicle number 18. Under the "3A" is the bridging weight circle. (USA/Green)

(Above) This M4 has all of its codes in the middle section of the three-piece transmission cover, like the markings on the M3A1 in the first photograph of this section. This was an unusual application by 1943. The Sherman is from Company B, 13th Armored Regiment, of the 1st Armored Division in Italy. (USA/NA)

(Below) This M4A3 Dozer Tank carries its codes on the back of the turret due to the extra rack added by the crew on the rear. This is one of the more unusual placements of the codes. Although the 12th Armored Division designator can be seen, the first number of the 23rd Armored Regiment is hidden by a strap. (USA/NA)

(Above) This M8 armored car carries a rarely seen bumper code on a solid white background that also includes a unit crest. It is from the 5th Army, 91st Armored Reconnaissance Squadron, Company A, and is vehicle 49. The name "ARGONAUGHT" on the side follows the practice of using names beginning with the company letter. It appears the vehicle has been painted in a camouflage of Earth Brown over Olive Drab. The small star with the wide circle was very common in the Italian theater of operation. The nine-ton yellow bridging classification is on the side fender guard. (USA/NA)

(Below) This M2 Halftrack has its bar on the upper right corner of a box attached to the rear. The horizontal bars to the side are a unit identification marking consisting of colored bars outlined in white. The crewman to the right in the leather jacket is Jack Pennick, a World War I Marine who served in the Navy Reserve during World War II. He was a character actor who played a cavalry sergeant in several John Ford movies with John Wayne. What a sailor is doing in the desert near Souk el Khemis in November 1942 is an interesting question. (USA/PAM)

(Above) This jeep carries its bumper markings on an actual bumper. It is from the 4th Armored Division, 66th Field Artillery Battalion, assigned to the Headquarters unit, and is vehicle 11 in the unit. Field Artillery was indicated by either an "F" or an "FA." The non-regulation fender extensions have stars painted on both of them. (USA/NA)

(Below) The 1st Armored Division used a complicated series of geometric symbols to identify tank battalions within its regiments. This M3 has its markings painted on the 75mm gun sponson. It is from the 13th Armored Regiment which used a bar with a square, while its sister regiment, the 1st, used a bar with a circle. The angle of the bar indicated which battalion the tank was from. All the markings except the blue drab serial numbers are in yellow. (USA/NA)

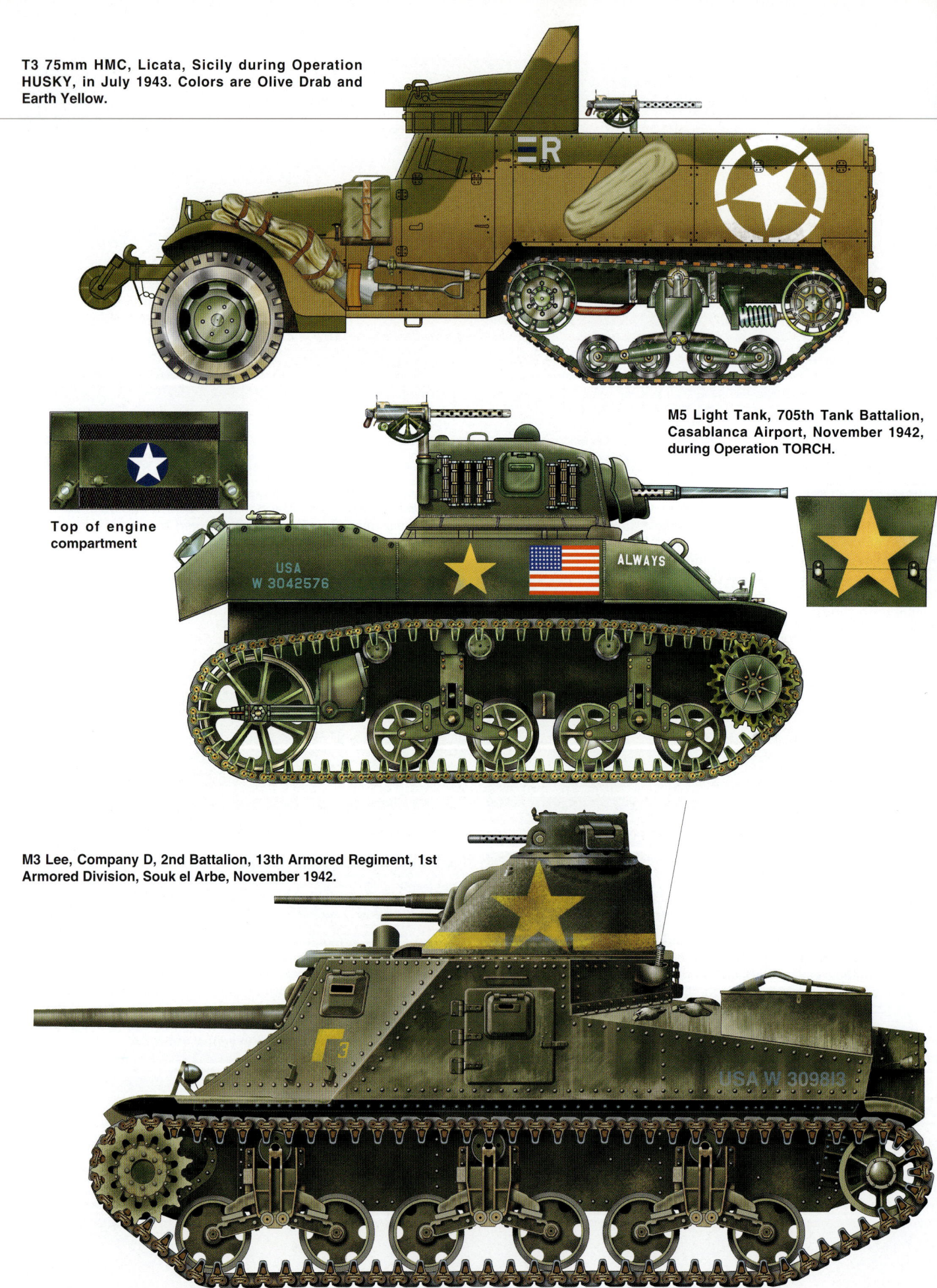

T3 75mm HMC, Licata, Sicily during Operation HUSKY, in July 1943. Colors are Olive Drab and Earth Yellow.

M5 Light Tank, 705th Tank Battalion, Casablanca Airport, November 1942, during Operation TORCH.

Top of engine compartment

M3 Lee, Company D, 2nd Battalion, 13th Armored Regiment, 1st Armored Division, Souk el Arbe, November 1942.

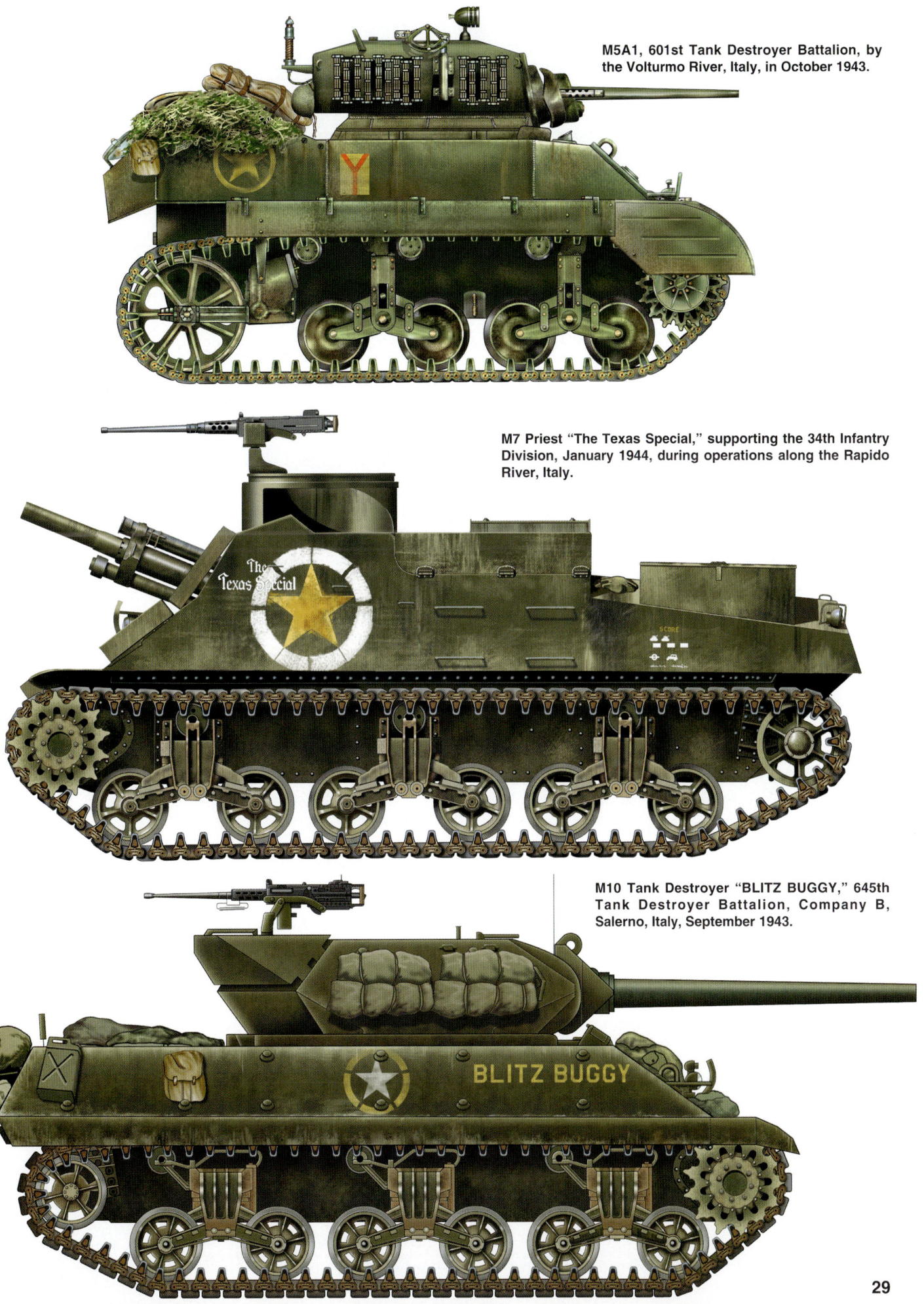

M5A1, 601st Tank Destroyer Battalion, by the Volturmo River, Italy, in October 1943.

M7 Priest "The Texas Special," supporting the 34th Infantry Division, January 1944, during operations along the Rapido River, Italy.

M10 Tank Destroyer "BLITZ BUGGY," 645th Tank Destroyer Battalion, Company B, Salerno, Italy, September 1943.

(Above) The 2nd Armored Division used a series of thin horizontal bars for their tactical markings. This M4A1 has a small bar underneath its name preceded by a "T," the identification for the 67th Armored Regiment. The 66th Armored Regiment used squares on its bars. This tank carries a camouflage pattern of Earth Yellow over Olive Drab and features the prominent circle and star markings that were first used during Operation HUSKY, the invasion of Sicily. (USA/NA)

(Below) The 6th Armored Division made use of large triangles or squares on the sides of the hull for a period of time. Eventually these were painted out as being too conspicuous, and large tactical numbers were substituted. This M4 from the 68th Tank Battalion carries both on its whitewashed sides. (USA/NA)

(Above) During the Normandy Campaign the 2nd Armored Division began applying wide bands of black paint over its vehicles' Olive Drab. In addition, large tactical letters and numbers in yellow were added, as seen on this M8 armored car during the advance across France in the summer of 1944. The name "COLBERT" conforms to the practice of using the company letter for the first letter in the name. (USA/NA)

(Below) During the Normandy Campaign the 3rd Armored Division painted large yellow tactical numbers on the sides of its tanks. This M5A1 is from Company "C" of the 33rd Armored Regiment. The name "CAROL" begins with the company letter. All markings are in white except for the tactical numbers and letter. (USA/PAM)

(Above) The 11th Armored Division painted large tactical numbers on their hull sides, often very roughly. These stand out fairly well, yet the hull stars have been painted out as being too conspicuous. (USA/NA)

(Below) The 14th Armored Division often painted their codes on their barrels, the only unit to use this system. This was due to the fact that no room was available elsewhere because of supplemental armor and equipment. (USA/NA)

(Above) The 12th Armored Division used a series of chevrons and horizontal bars on the sides of their hulls to designate the battalion. An upward chevron denoted the 23rd, a horizontal bar denoted the 43rd, and a downward chevron as shown here denoted the 714th tank battalion. The company letter was at the top, and dots on either side signified the platoon. (USA/PAM)

(Below) The 11th Armored Division also used red bands on the turret and hull star arms to denote the battalion late in the war. Bands on the 12 o'clock arm indicated the 22nd Tank Battalion, bands on the 7 o'clock arm indicated the 41st Tank Battalion, and the 9 o'clock arm was used by the 42nd Tank Battalion. The number of bands indicated the company, and the number of dots the platoon. This M4A3E8 is from the 41st Tank Battalion, Company F, 1st Platoon. (USA/NA)

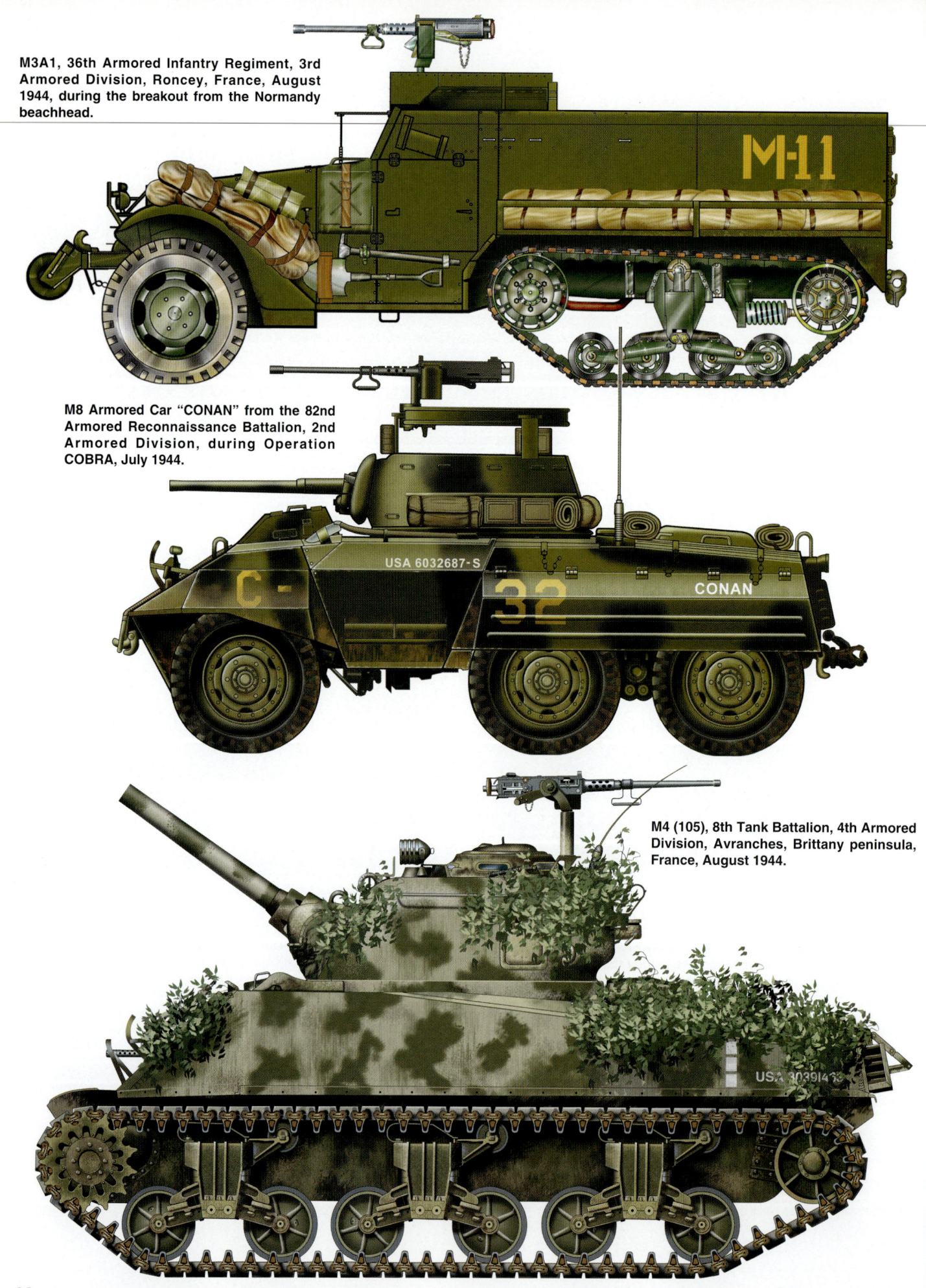

M3A1, 36th Armored Infantry Regiment, 3rd Armored Division, Roncey, France, August 1944, during the breakout from the Normandy beachhead.

M8 Armored Car "CONAN" from the 82nd Armored Reconnaissance Battalion, 2nd Armored Division, during Operation COBRA, July 1944.

M4 (105), 8th Tank Battalion, 4th Armored Division, Avranches, Brittany peninsula, France, August 1944.

M4 (105), 6th Armored Division, during a fire mission near Trois Vierge, Luxembourg, January 24th, 1945.

M12, "ALBERTA IV," 11th Armored Division, near Rudesheim, Germany, March 1945.

M4A3(76) W, 19th Tank Battalion, 9th Armored Division, Belgium, November 1944.

(Above) The first American employment of tanks in the European Theater occurred in North Africa during the "TORCH" invasion. Little thought was given to camouflage at the time, and the American tankers in their Olive Drab tanks, like this M3 "Lee," stood out against the lighter-colored soil as they advanced into Tunisia. This M3 is from the 13th Armored Regiment, 1st Armored Division, near Souk el Khemis. (USA/NA)

(Above) With no paint for camouflage, tankers used mud to help break up the silhouette of their vehicles. This M3 halftrack has a roughly applied coat of mud. (USA/PAM)

(Below) This T28E1 CGMC features a swirl pattern of mud smeared on all the surfaces, including the ammunition cans. The use of foliage and the extra gear carried by the crew also helps break up the outline of the vehicle. (USA/PAM)

(Below) By comparison, the crew of this M3 has covered their half-track in large splotches and bands to break up its silhouette. Both this and the vehicle pictured above are from the 1st Armored Division. (USA/PAM)

(Above) This M6 37mm GMC has a particularly rough mud application on its gun shield. In addition the large star on the side of the truck has been covered with mud to tone it down making it less conspicuous. The wide variation of patterns on these vehicles was due to the whims of the crews, as no guidance came from higher command.

(Below) This victory parade at the conclusion of the North African campaign featured numerous M3 halftracks, all painted in Olive Drab and Tan/Earth Yellow. Careful scrutiny shows that none of the patterns match, indicating that there was no official pattern used when the vehicles were painted for the parade. (USA/NA)

(Below) Operation HUSKY, the invasion of Sicily in July 1943, was the first time that OM34 was put into practice in combat. This T2, "GO GET IT" from the 3rd Armored Division, sits in an LCT with a two-tone camouflage scheme of Earth Yellow over Olive Drab. It also has a small star in a circle, the first time this type of marking was used in the Mediterranean Theater of operation. (USA/NA)

(Below) This M7 lacks the circle and star markings on its side, but does carry an Earth Yellow over Olive Drab camouflage pattern. The combination of painted camouflage, vegetation, and netting helped vehicles to blend in well with the surrounding terrain. However, little could be done to mask the smoke from gunfire except the use of smokeless powder. (USA/NA)

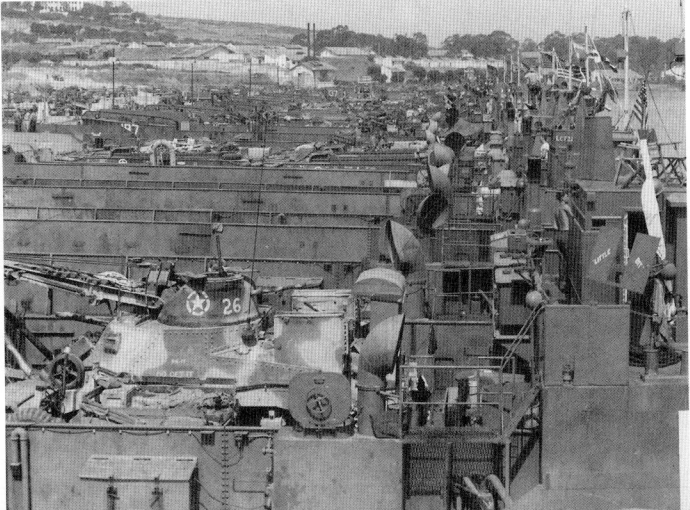

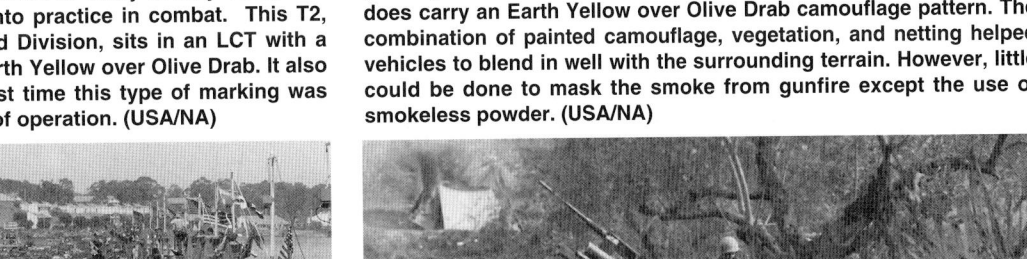

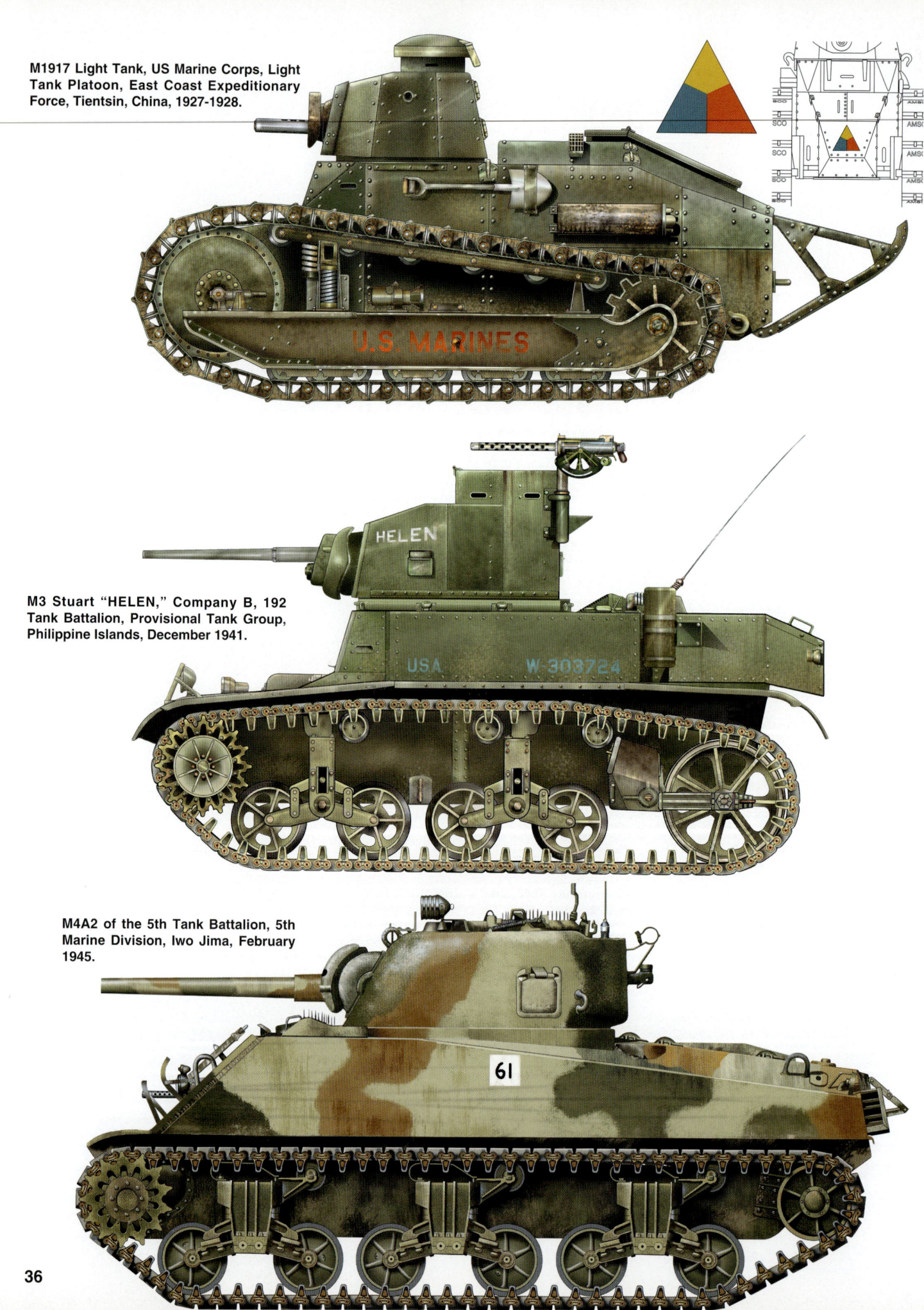

M1917 Light Tank, US Marine Corps, Light Tank Platoon, East Coast Expeditionary Force, Tientsin, China, 1927-1928.

M3 Stuart "HELEN," Company B, 192 Tank Battalion, Provisional Tank Group, Philippine Islands, December 1941.

M4A2 of the 5th Tank Battalion, 5th Marine Division, Iwo Jima, February 1945.

"COLORADO" of Company C, 1st Marine Amphibious Corps Tank Battalion, 3rd Platoon, Betio Island, Tarawa Atoll, November, 1943.

M4A2, Marine 2nd Separate Tank Company, Guam, July 1944.

M4 composite hull flamethrower of the 713th Tank Battalion during fighting on Okinawa.

(Above) One of the more interesting innovations was the use of counter-shading to help break up the silhouette of a vehicle. This M7 has had its lower hull painted white to help avoid or lessen the effects of shadows caused by darker colors in the shade. This type of counter-shading was tried on several types of vehicles but never saw widespread use. (USA/NA)

(Below) This M31 ARV features a unique four-color camouflage scheme that appears to consist of Olive Drab, Black, Earth Red or Brown, and Earth Yellow. Units such as this had access to paint and spray equipment and thus were able, if time was available, to devote more effort to camouflaging their vehicles. (USA/NA)

(Above) This M4 features counter-shading on its lower hull and under its gun barrel. It also has a pattern of Black over its Olive Drab base, although Earth Red could also be used. This tank is from the 13th Regiment of the 1st Armored Division and is the tank of the "F" Company commander of the 2nd Battalion. (USA/PAM)

(Below) Although there were official patterns, some rather innovative schemes evolved as the result of individual efforts. This M8 GMC carries a wavy disruptive scheme of what appears to be Earth Yellow over Olive Drab in Italy, late 1943. (USA/NA)

(Above) Earth Brown over the Olive Drab base also began to appear in 1944. This dug-in M4's camouflage pattern would be more effective with the use of foliage and netting, particularly in the open like this. (USA/NA)

(Below) Late in the war, Black began to be used in wide swaths over the Olive Drab base. This M4A3E8 has had Black sprayed in random patterns over it, including the sandbag supplemental armor. Painting was often done as quickly as possible with little regard for neatness or what was being painted. (USA/NA )

(Above) During fighting in France the 8th Battalion of the 4th Armored Division extensively camouflaged their vehicles with mud and foliage. They also used an upright bar on the hull side to indicate the platoon. This bar can barely be seen just in front of the serial number and is segmented into three sections for the 3rd Platoon. (USA/PAM)

(Below) The winter of 1944-1945 saw the extensive camouflage of Army vehicles throughout Europe. Paint, lime, and salt were used to help cover up the Olive Drab finish of many vehicles to help them blend in better against the white backdrop. Thin bands of Olive Drab were to be left so the vehicles could blend into forest areas. This M10 has vertical stripes of Olive Drab to help it blend in with a tree line. (USA/NA)

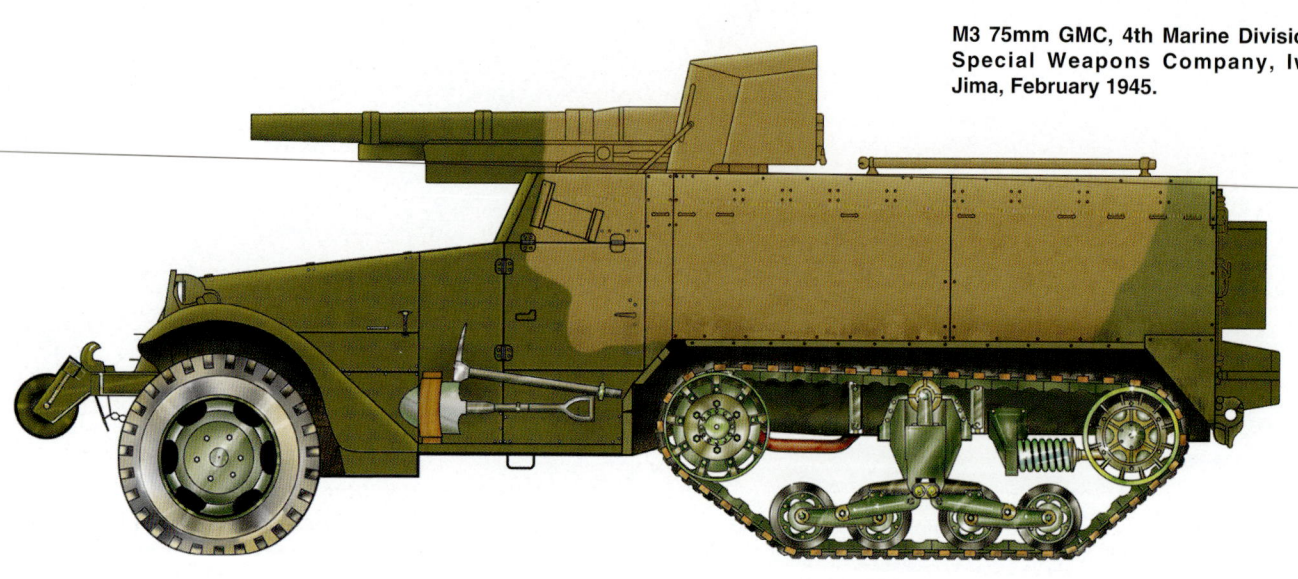

M3 75mm GMC, 4th Marine Division, Special Weapons Company, Iwo Jima, February 1945.

M7 Priest, Special Weapons Company, 22nd Marine Regiment, Oraku Peninsula, Okinawa in June 1945.

LTV(A)-2, Yellow Beach, Iwo Jima, February 1945.

(Above) Like the photo in the Introduction, this also illustrates how painting was often done. This soldier has thrown a bucket of white color onto the bogey unit of an M36. Often troops used mops, rags, or threw it on like this to quickly camouflage their vehicles. The lime and salt were often mixed to make a thick whitewash that was easy to apply. Complete and neat coverage was not the goal in most cases — just get it on and do it as quickly as possible! (USA/NA)

(Below) Most vehicles did not have bands of Olive Drab left on the vehicle as most troops were more concerned with getting the vehicle's base Olive Drab color covered up. This was fine if the vehicle was in the open like this M36 in Luxembourg. But against a tree line the solid White could stand out unless covered with camouflage netting or foliage. (USA/NA)

(Above) This M2A1 halftrack has also had vertical stripes of Olive Drab left on it, and the effect is quite convincing as it moves down a road in Belgium. The Olive Drab bands help break up its silhouette against the background foliage instead of presenting a big white object that would stand out against trees. (USA/PAM)

(Below) These M4s of the 40th Tank Battalion, 7th Armored Division at St. Vith illustrate how a solid White camouflage tank stands out against a tree line. The tank in the foreground with the camouflage netting on its side blends in better but could still benefit from more netting or foliage to help break up its silhouette. (USA/NA)

(Above) If some sort of paint or whitewash was not available some crews resorted to white cloth to help break up their vehicle's outline. This M18 crew has wrapped a sheet around the gun barrel and over part of the canvas mantlet cover in an effort to cut down the Olive Drab's contrast against the snow. The snow atop the sandbags on the front hull has further helped to break up the vehicle's outline when viewed from a head-on position. (USA/NA)

(Above) Whitewash did not hold up well under field conditions. Crew movement and the elements quickly gave most vehicles a rather scruffy appearance. As often as not only the upper hull and turrets of AFVs were painted, but the lower hull and bogie wheels were quickly covered with mud, and it was felt painting them was a waste of time. (USA/NA)

(Below) Camouflage could be carried to the extreme as shown here where even the blade of this dozer M4 has been painted. It also illustrates how quickly dirt, mud, water and wear can destroy the camouflage effect. The unit codes on the hull just below the drivers' positions have been moved up to this location, as the dozer attachment made seeing them difficult. (USA/NA)

(Above) By comparison with the last photo this dozer M4 has a much more neatly applied whitewash scheme. This shows just how much variation occurred with the whitewash application between different units. (USA/NA)

(Above) Some crews left codes, serial numbers, and stars visible when camouflaging their vehicles, as the crew of this M8 armored car has done. Camouflage was more consistent when done by depots and varied far more when done by individual crews. (USA/PAM)

(Below) One of the more interesting snow camouflage schemes was the one on this M4A3 (76) from the 709th Tank Battalion in support of 75th Infantry Division near Colmar, France, in early 1945. The crew has used an irregular pattern of bands and squiggles to break up the outline of their vehicle. (USA/PAM)

(Above) This M10 carried an unusual scheme of broad bands of White and Olive Drab on its side and turret in Italy in February, 1945. This type of broad pattern was rarely seen. (USA/NA)

(Above) Perhaps the most extensive whitewash camouflage was carried out by M29 "Weasel" units. This M29 displays an intricate and extensive camouflage scheme using a pattern of Olive Drab and Black to help break up the silhouette of this light tracked amphibious cargo carrier. (USA/NA)

(Below) Not all vehicles received whitewash camouflage, but those that didn't could still be effectively concealed. This was particularly true of artillery units that had access to camouflage netting. The snowfall on the vehicle and the netting has helped the M7 blend in well on the flat terrain. (USA/NA)

# VEHICLE NAMES AND PERSONAL MARKINGS

The use of names on vehicles never received official sanction aside from those used in conjunction with the company letter. It was common for units using this pattern to have all their vehicles' names begin with the letter of the company. Aside from this practice it was rare to see other names applied to a tank or vehicle, unlike the practice that was extremely common with aircraft. This was larglely due to the fact that crews had little access to paint and even less time to devote to painting names on their vehicles. This was especially true the closer one came to the front, since crews had to rearm, service, and carry out preventive maintenance on their vehicles before they could eat, take care of personal needs, and sleep. Naming their vehicles was not high on their priority list.

Some names were carried along as the crew received new vehicles to replace old or destroyed ones. When this was done a number was usually added at the end to indicate how many vehicles the crew had gone through. This was especially practiced by Colonel Creighton Abrams with his series of tanks named "THUNDERBOLT," at least seven of which he commanded.

G.I.s being what they were, names painted on vehicles reflected a whole series of items. Of course many names were of girl friends. Some names carried a sort of macabre sense of humor, something that troops, especially those in combat, used to underscore their sometimes dangerous existence or poke fun at things around them. Occasionally more elaborate artwork, ranging from pinups to cartoons, would appear on vehicles. Some of these were quite elaborate, but they were the exception rather then the rule. Some markings were temporarily applied with chalk under special circumstances. This might havebe done by villagers who were liberated or to highlight a particularly successful mission. In general, however, it was not a common practice for tanks and vehicles to carry markings outside those normally sanctioned by higher officials.

(Left) A long-barreled M3 Lee of the 1st Armored Division on a training exercise in Northern Ireland prior to "OPERATION TORCH." The Name "STUD" is reflected in the drawing of a horse on the hull side. The horse's head appears to have been drawn in chalk. The blue drab registration number is barely visible at the rear on the hull side. (USA/ Hunnicutt)

(Below) "KENTUCKY," an M3 from the 1st Armored Division in North Africa. The markings on the tank are in yellow except for the blue drab registration number. The "L" under the side vision port indicates Company "F." These type of markings were used by the 13th Armored Regiment. (USA/ PAM)

The crew of this M3 admire a photo of a pretty girl taped to the side of their tank below her name. Obviously any photo attached like this would quickly come off or be ruined which suggests that this is more of a publicity photograph rather then an actual personal marking. (USA/ PAM)

"BULL O THE WOODS" slid off the side of the road in Italy and is in the process of being retrieved. This name probably reflects the crew's choice rather than one used in conjunction with a company letter. (USA/NA)

"ALLEY OOP III" is an example of a crew that has gone through at least two other vehicles of the same name. Though not a common practice, this naming and numbering of vehicles did occasionally appear. (USA/NA)

(Above) "OLD MUD & RUTS" is obviously a take-off on General George Patton's nickname, "Old Blood & Guts." G.I.s had a way of being irreverent or sarcastic that was hard to suppress. (USA/PAM)

(Below) This M4A3E2 was the first tank into Bastogne as part of Patton's relief drive to the encircled garrison. The name was chalked on the side and the registration numbers were enlarged. The original name, "COBRA KING," is under "BASTOGNE." (USA/PAM)

(Above) "STUKU BAITE" is an example of the macabre sense of humor troops exhibited on the battlefield, a hallmark of American soldiers since earliest times. (USA/PAM)

(Below) Elaborate cartoons were seldom seen on tanks, but "BELLE OF LITTLE ROCK" was an exception. It depicts Uncle Sam chasing Hitler. Barely visible behind Uncle Sam is the white star with a yellow surround. This tank was from Company "B," 755th Tank Battalion, in Italy in May 1944. (USA/NA)

# US ARMY ARMOR - PACIFIC

The Army deployed two National Guard tank battalions, the 192nd and the 194th, to reinforce the Philippines in late 1941. Also sent were 50 M3 75mm GMC halftracks to act as mobile artillery. All these vehicles were painted Olive Drab overall and carried Blue Drab registration numbers. There were no tactical markings carried, although several tanks in the 192nd carried names in white on the turret sides. There were also 57 Bren gun carriers taken over when they were unable to be shipped to the British garrison at Hong Kong after the outbreak of hostilities. Nothing has surfaced about their color or markings, and they remain an elusive part of the history of the Philippine campaign.

As the U.S. slowly built up its strength in the Pacific to counter the Japanese, both light and medium tanks began to arrive. Unlike the European Theater, there were no large armored formations in the Pacific. Normally the largest would be a battalion, although more often tanks operated in company strength. During several of the island campaigns later in the war, notably in the Philippines and Okinawa, there were larger concentrations of tank and tank destroyer units comparable to armored divisions in Europe.

The markings for Army vehicles in the Pacific did not differ significantly in general patterns from their European counterparts. The use of stars was very common, but as fighting progressed many of these were painted over, as they were felt to be good aiming points for Japanese gunners. Registration numbers first appeared in Blue Drab, but as the war progressed these changed to the more common white. There was an interesting difference in the Pacific that was not practiced in Europe. Several units painted the legend "U.S. ARMY" instead of "USA" by their registration numbers. Why this occurred has not surfaced though there is the suggestion that the Army troops did not want to be misidentified as Marines!

Bumper codes followed the same pattern as in Europe, although they were not as complex due to the small number of units in the Pacific. Many units did not even apply bumper codes since they operated so often in small numbers. A more common type of marking system adopted was the use of large tactical numbers, normally on the side of a tank turret. Another practice used in both theaters and also by the Marines was the use of names beginning with the company letter.

An interesting way to deal with security developed by allowing individual units to devise their own tactical markings, which could be altered or changed entirely from one campaign to the next in order to confuse the Japanese. Some interesting and unique markings resulted from this practice. These included varied geometric designs, dice combinations, chevrons, bars, and flag poles painted on hull sides.

Camouflage was used on a limited scale but rarely approached the complexity that appeared on some Marine vehicles. Normally it consisted of bands of color sprayed over the Olive Drab base coat. There were some exceptions to this practice, such as the complex schemes carried on some DUKWs supporting the Marines at Iwo Jima.

Due to the small numbers of armored units compared to the European Theater, U.S. armor camouflage and markings in the Pacific never received the attention they received in Europe. Much was left to individual units, and this resulted in some unique and interesting schemes, especially as the war progressed into the final year.

**The first use of American armor in combat was in the Philippines, where two battalions of M3 light tanks, 50 T12 GMCs, 46 M2 and M3 halftracks, and some British Bren gun carriers saw action. From the little photographic evidence that is available, these carried only serial numbers, although at least one M3 had a name on it. This T12 sits hidden in a field during the retreat to Bataan. (Green)**

(Above) These Marmon-Herrington T14 (front) and T16 (rear) light tanks were used on Umnak Island in Alaska. From the 602nd Independent Tank Company, they have a yellow band and star around the turrets. They were photographed in June 1942 around the time of the battle of Midway, when Japanese forces made a diversionary attack on the Aleutians. (USA/NA)

(Below) White stars were also carried prominently toward the rear of the turret. The legend "LCM-4" is written on the side of the hull in chalk for pre-positioning purposes. Underneath it in Blue Drab is the serial number "U.S.A. W-3013473." (USA/PAM)

(Above) As part of the invasion of Tarawa, Army forces landed on Makin Island with M3 Lees and M3A1 light tanks. The light tanks were from the 193rd Tank Battalion and had large white numbers toward the front of the turret. (USA/NA)

(Below) On the left rear of the tanks was a yellow triangle with a red square in it, the battalion insignia. On the right was the company letter and the individual tank number. (USA/NA)

(Above) The Army also used a small number of LVTs during the Makin invasion. This particular one carried a large white star on its sponson with an unusual border around it. (USA/NA)

(Below) This M4A1 of the 603rd Tank Company in support of the 41st Infantry Division during fighting in the Admiralty Islands in March 1944 has been camouflaged with broad bands of Brown or Earth Red over Olive Drab. A small tactical number is visible on the bottom of the turret along with the name "SLOPPY JOE" on the hull side. It does not appear that the tank has even the remnants of a white star. (USA/NA)

(Above) These M4A1's from the 767th Tank Battalion move across the beach on Kwajelein atoll in February 1944. They are fully marked with large stars and tactical markings on the turret and hull, along with names on the forward part of the hull side. The first tank, "LUCKY TIGER," is followed by "MISS DINAH." (USA/NA)

(Below) The crews of these M4s have painted out the white stars. On the rear corners of the hull are circles which contained a tactical number. These tanks are from the 754th Tank Battalion on Bougainville in March 1944. In the Pacific, local commanders often devised their own tactical markings. (USA/NA)

(Above) "COGNAC" and "CUPID," composite hull M4s, move up through Agana, Guam, in August 1944. It appears their hull and turret stars have been painted out. The legend "US ARMY" instead of "USA" in conjunction with the serial numbers was peculiar to armor units in the Pacific. The use of names beginning with "C" would be indicative of "C" Company, further proof of which is the letter "C" just barely visible on the transmission cover of "CUPID." (USA/NA)

(Below) "MAN O WAR," an M4A1, appears to have had its name painted on a darker background then the faded Olive Drab, or the dust was wiped away to make it stand out. Either way, the name contrasts vividly against the hull. A rarely seen feature is the use of grousers on the smooth track blocks for additional traction in the muddy conditions of Leyte. (USA/PAMS)

(Above) During the Philippine invasion many tanks carried large stars on their engine decks to prevent accidental attack by U.S. aircraft. This star can easily be seen on the rear of this composite hull M4. Less visible is the smaller star next to the commander's hatch, partially hidden by the open hatch. (USA/PAM/Green)

(Below) "BUSHMASTER," a composite hull Sherman, is from the 763rd Tank Battalion. Both tanks carry the complete "US ARMY" legend on their rear hull sides, although the serial number is not visible on "BUSHMASTER," having been painted out or covered with dirt. (USA/NA)

(Above) An M4A1 from the 754th Tank Battalion moves through Manila following the invasion of Luzon. On Bougainville this unit had its tactical numbers located on the rear of the hull, but in the Philippines the markings have been moved forward. (USA/NA)

(Below) "SUPER RABBIT," an M7 Priest, moves through a town on Panay in March 1945. Aside from the name and the star on the early three-piece transmission housing, no other markings are visible. The M7 first saw widespread use by the Army in the Pacific during the Philippine invasion. (USA/NA)

(Above) This composite hull M4 from the 44th Tank Battalion moves through Manila. The lines on the side of the applique armor are part of a series of geometric markings used by this battalion in the Philippine campaign. (USA/PAM/Green)

(Below) The 775th Tank Battalion must have had paint, time, and a talented artist, as these M4s feature names, dice, and some well painted "nudes" on their hulls. While the dice are on the front applique armor, the exact placement of the names and nudes varies from tank to tank. The dice numbers may be the tank's tactical number although this is only an educated guess. Completely absent is any indication of serial number or stars. (USA/NA)

(Above) This M4A3, "CLASSY PEG" from the 716th Tank Battalion, passes a destroyed Japanese Type 97-kai Shinhoto Chi-ha of the 2nd Armored Division. On the side of the hull in front of the name is an elaborate wolf's head, possibly from a Walt Disney cartoon. (USA/NA)

(Below) This LVT(A)-1 moves up to provide support for the 96th Infantry Division. It carries prominent registration numbers and stars on the rear hull and turret. On the turret's rear are painted white shamrocks that may be tactical or battalion markings. (USA/NA)

(Below) This M8 armored car carries the prominent legend "US ARMY" on both the hull side and rear. This type of marking was seen on most types of armored vehicles used by the Army in the Pacific Theater. (USA/NAP)

(Above) The famous writer Ernie Pyle was killed during the fighting on Ie Shima, and this M7 self-propelled gun was named in his honor. An unusual modification has been the addition of a .30-caliber machine gun above the drivers compartment to supplement the pulpit mounted .50-caliber machine gun. (USA/NA)

(Below) These composite hull flame throwers and 105-equipped howitzer tanks have had their hull stars painted out in various ways. While some of the crews have followed the general outline of the star, several, including the one on the left, have just covered them over in any fashion. (USA/NA)

(Above) This flame thrower M4 is from the 713th Tank Battalion as indicated on the rear hull. The tactical number on the turret has also been painted on the rear hull. (USA/NA)

(Below) This composite hull flame thrower has had its stars painted out on the hull side and taped over on the turret. The prominent "US ARMY" is visible on the rear hull. (USA/NA)

# US MARINE CORPS ARMOR

The Marine Corps did not use tanks during World War I. In 1923 it formed its first tank platoon with FT-17s borrowed from the Army. This platoon was used during amphibious exercises and also acquired more tanks from the Army. In 1927 it deployed to China for fifteen months to reinforce American forces there. It was disbanded upon its return and the tanks put into storage.

The FT-17s were painted Olive Drab, and some retained the old three-color Tank Corps insignia. Some eventually had the Marine Corps insignia on their front armor and the inscription "U.S. MARINES" on the road wheel suspension rail in red.

During the late 1930s the Marines looked at the Marmon-Herrington CTL-3 light tank for use in amphibious operations. Several versions of Marmon-Herrington light tanks were procured. These were painted Olive Drab and carried tactical markings based on the Army system of geometric shapes for platoons. None of these ever saw combat, although some were used in the early days of World War II on American Samoa.

As war grew imminent the Marines began to acquire M2A4 and M3 light tanks. In the summer of 1941 the Marines occupied Iceland, and this force included Company A, 2nd Tank Battalion, 10th Marine Regiment, minus one platoon. This was the first combat deployment of Marines Corps armor since the 1927 expedition to China.

When the Japanese attacked Pearl Harbor on December 7th, 1941, the Marines, like the Army, were woefully under-equipped with tanks. Throughout the early days of the war the Marines slowly acquired more M2A4s, M3s, and M3A1s as American industry began to increase its tank production. The first combat experience for Marine Corps tankers occurred during the Battle of Midway in June 1942. A platoon of M3s was sent to the island as reinforcements, and during the air attack the crews fired their turret-mounted machine guns at any Japanese aircraft that came in range. The tanks received by the Marines were painted in standard Army Olive Drab, but there are several photos of M3s painted in a sand color. Although not specifically identified, these may have been at Midway and would be the first examples of camouflage used on Marine Corps tanks in the war.

## The Solomons

Marine Corps tanks next saw action during the invasion of Guadalcanal in August 1942. Both M2A4s and M3s were used by the 1st Marine Tank Battalion. These carried a variety of markings. A mixture of Army and Marine Corps markings were carried demonstrating their mixed origins. The battalion did use geometric shapes and bands to identify their platoons and companies. Stars were also carried, but these were not in the standard pattern that was common on Army tanks at that time. There is at least one photo of an M2A4 with a star on its turret in what appears to be a blue surround similar to the markings carried by American aircraft at the time. Halftracks also saw limited service on Guadalcanal, but these appeared to carry no specific markings other than registration numbers. All these vehicles were in the standard Olive Drab overall. The Marines did employ the LVT-1 to move supplies through the muddy terrain. These were painted Ocean Gray overall, probably due to their procurement under a Navy contract.

Following the Guadalcanal campaign, Allied forces moved further up the Solomons chain. The Marines still employed the M3A1 but also received new M4A2 medium tanks. Markings were fairly nondescript, with few tanks if any marked with stars. Some geometric symbols were used for platoon and company identification. The notable exception to this was the 3rd Marine Tank Battalion, which marked its M3A1s with geometric symbols, names, and nudes. This was the rare exception to what were fairly limited and mundane markings for the majority of the Solomons campaign. Camouflage began to appear, in particular on the M3 75mm GMC halftracks, which featured some unique patterns. These seem to have been applied by their crews without any official instructions to follow. Newer M5s also began to appear to replace the older M3 series, and some of these were also camouflaged in random patterns of Field Drab or Brown over the standard Olive Drab.

## Island Hopping

While the campaign in the Solomons was being waged, moves were underway in the Central Pacific to capture Japanese islands for advanced bases. The first of these was the Tarawa atoll of Betio, where the 2nd Marine Division carried out one of the most bloody assaults of the Pacific war. Here the Marines employed LVT-1s and -2s to carry troops over the outer reef. These were painted in the standard Ocean Grey, and many carried both names and large numbers. Some of these numbers were painted on white backgrounds while others were painted in white against the Ocean Grey background. Some these were neatly stenciled while others were quite crudely done. Some of the LVTs carried stars, and in at least one case the star was upside down on the front of an LVT-1. This may have been done deliberately for aerial recognition. In addition to the amtracs the Marines also employed M4A2s in the initial assault and M3A1s on the second day of the battle. These were painted standard Olive Drab. The M4A2s all carried names beginning with "C" and the unit insignia, an elephant with a smoking trunk and blanket over its back. The light tanks used geometric insignias and names to denote companies. It does not appear that any of these tanks carried stars.

The assault on the Marshall Islands followed Tarawa. Tanks had proved their worth at Tarawa, especially the M4s. By this time camouflage was becoming more common, and both light and medium tanks carried a variety of camouflage patterns. Names of vehicles usually began with the company letter, and geometric symbols were common for company identification. Wooden planks on the sides of M4s also made their first appearance to counter the use of magnetic mines by suicidal Japanese infantry.

The Marshalls were followed up by the invasion of Saipan, Tinian, and Guam by Army and Marine troops. By this time the Marines were predominantly using the M4A2. Camouflage was becoming more evident along with some distinctive markings for specific units, but stars were still not common. The 3rd Tank Battalion did use a winged star, similar to that used on American aircraft, but this was more the exception than the rule. The 4th Tank Battalion painted the tops of their M4s' turrets white with large red numbers to help to better coordinate air strikes. Geometric symbols and names still were fairly consistent to identify companies. Some tanks carried personal names that did not reflect the company letter, and some crews took to placing their names near their crew positions.

**(Below) The first Marine Corps tank unit was a platoon of M1917 light tanks borrowed from the Army. In April 1927 the platoon was shipped to China where it spent over a year. Shipped home in September 1928, the unit was disbanded and its tanks placed in storage. This M1917 is being loaded on a transport for China. A Tank Corps emblem is on the nose of the hull just below the driver's hatches. (USMC/NA)**

By this stage in the war the amphibious tractors were also starting to be camouflaged. To help with beach assembly they also began to carry vertical stripes on their sides and on occasion their fronts and rears. The color of the stripes indicated the beach, and the number of stripes the specific beach. For example, two blue stripes would indicate Blue Beach 2. These were intended to help the tractors locate their units and find their assigned beaches more easily, but in the confusion of an amphibious assault, units often became intermixed and landed on different beaches. Armored LVTs used for support often carried the company letter in conjunction with the vehicle number.

**Iwo Jima and Okinawa**

The Marines' bloodiest campaign began 19 February 1945, when three Marine Divisions landed on the island of Iwo Jima. Backing them up were three tank battalions of M4A2s, the 3rd, 4th, and 5th. Each in their own way were distinctively marked. The 3rd carried the winged star and bar insignia on their tanks' sides and on the turret tops. Tactical or "speed" numbers were often carried on the gun mantlet. Often a small diamond insignia was seen with an identification number inside the diamond. This unit did not add supplemental armor in the form of planks, concrete and sandbags as did the other two battalions. The 4th used a semicircle for its identification and normally placed large tactical numbers on the sides of their tanks along with a name in smaller letters. It appears that some but not all their tanks were also camouflaged. The 5th used a three-color camouflage pattern on most if not all its tanks. Most did not carry a name. A small square with a number inside was used for identification. Amphibious tractors and amtanks used the same series of markings that had been developed during the invasion of the Marianas

**(Above)** This diesel-powered M3 features a more neatly applied star with a white band around the lower turret. The old Army serial number in Blue Drab is barely discernable on the hull side. The tank is from Company "C" of the 1st Marine Tank Battalion on Guadalcanal. (USMC/NA)

the previous summer. The venerable M3 75mm GMCs that were still in the weapons company were camouflaged in wide bands. Many of the support and supply vehicles and some artillery were also camouflaged.

The campaign for Okinawa did not produce any unusual markings or camouflage patterns. The introduction of new equipment such as the M7 "Priest" resulted in the retirement of the M3 75mm GMC. The M7s saw extensive service in direct support and often had extensive amounts of spare track for supplemental armor. Many of the M7s also received a camouflage pattern of Sand over their base Olive Drab color.

**(Below)** This M3 moves along a road on Guadalcanal. The placement of the star off-center on the front hull is unusual. It also appears to be in a blue circle similar to markings used in North Africa, but that may be because of the lighting. (USMC/NA)

**(Above)** The Marines were the only service to use the M2A4 in combat. This M2A4 is being unloaded for the landing at Guadalcanal in August 1942. In the early days of World War II the Marines rarely used the star insignia that was common on Army vehicles. The star on this tank was obviously painted freehand. There was a blue band around the top of the turret side, and the name "THE BLIZZARD" in white is on the pioneer tool guard on the hull side. (USMC/NA)

**(Below)** Guadalcanal also saw the first use of amphibious tractors in combat. Based on a design by John Roebling, the initial version, the LVT-1, was used to bring cargo ashore at Guadalcanal. These vehicles, unlike Marine tanks which were in Army Olive Drab, were painted in Navy Ocean Gray.

(Above) A new LVT-4 moves past a battleship shelling the Okinawa shoreline. It carries simple markings on the hull side, with the stripes on the rear for the beach identification. The LVT-4 featured a rear ramp that made unloading both simpler and safer than the early LVT-2s where the Marines had to jump over the sides. (USN/NA)

(Below) A dozer M4 with supplemental track armor on the turret and hull and planking over the suspension. On the right front hull are two markings, one of which appears to be a heart. The tank is from the 6th Tank Battalion at Naha. (USMC/NA)

(Above) A Sherman with an unusual waterproofing gun mantlet cover moves across a bridge. It carries both extra track and what appears to be planks reinforced by concrete on its side as supplemental armor. The extensive use of supplemental armor made it difficult to find a surface for markings. (USMC/NA)

(Below) At Okinawa the Marines used the M7 Priest for the first time. Many of these were fitted with extra track as supplemental armor on their thin sides. This M7 from the 29th Marine Regiment moves along a coastal road with a Marine squad on board as they drive toward the town of Ghuto. (USMC/NA)

Even artillery pieces were camouflaged. This 37mm cannon (above) with its usual shield carries what appears to be a three-color camouflage pattern. It is harder to distinguish from its background whether this 75mm pack howitzer (below) has a two- or three-color scheme. The colors are Sand or Earth Yellow and Red Brown on the Olive Drab base.

(Below) While Iwo Jima has always been thought of as a Marine Corps battle, Navy and Army personnel were also involved. This camouflaged DUKW disabled on the shore was from one of three Army DUKW companies that joined two Marine Corps companies in support of the operation. This vehicle exhibits the complete "US ARMY" legend on the side that was used by some units in the latter stages of the war. Following it is what appears to be either a unit or crew marking. (USMC/NA)

The numbers and names varied in size as can be seen on "CAIRO 41" when compared with the previous photos. The planks on the hull side were spaced out from the hull, and the cavity was filled with concrete for additional protection. The use of extra track links for protection was also common. (USMC/NA)

(Above) Camouflage was evident on vehicles used on Iwo Jima. This M3 75mm GMC carries a pattern of Earth Yellow or Sand and possibly Red Brown over the base coat of Olive Drab The Iwo Jima campaign was the last use of this support weapon by the marines in the war. (USMC/NA)

(Above and Below) Both of these trucks have been camouflaged in Earth Yellow or Sand over Olive Drab The truck above has become bogged down in the soft volcanic beach sand. The crew of this T45 4.5 inch multiple rocket launcher (below) prepares to fire their last remaining rockets. Once this is done their crews will quickly shift positions to avoid counter battery fire. (USMC/NA)

(Above) These LVTs show a variation in markings. The LVT-A4 on the left is in camouflage and has a name, company designation, and vehicle number on the rear. The center LVT-2 has two yellow stripes, a name on the armor plate, and the company and vehicle number on the front. The LVT-4 in the back has stripes on the side and rear ramp and possibly the company and vehicle number as well. (USMC/NA)

(Below) The two other tank battalions at Iwo Jima made extensive use of additional protection on the sides of their tanks. Large names and numbers were also used for identification such as seen on "COED 40." These markings were in yellow. (USMC/NA)

(Above) On Iwo Jima each division had a separate tank platoon for support. This M4A2 from the 3rd Tank Battalion carries the unit's unique star and bar marking virtually identical to the markings carried on Navy and Marine aircraft. Its tanks did not carry additional protection. The numbers on the turret were tactical markings for radio identification. (USMC/NA)

(Below) This LVT-A4 at Iwo Jima has a camouflage pattern similar to one in the previous photo but also has the single yellow stripe designating Yellow Beach 1 and the company letter and number on the upper side of the cargo hold and on the driver's glacis plate. A name also appears just at the upper edge of the side flotation section. (USMC/NA)

**(Above)** This M5A1 light tank of the 4th Marine Tank Battalion carries a rough camouflage paint scheme during the invasion of Namur in the Kwajalein Atoll in February 1944. The battalion insignia, a small semi-circle, can be seen on the hull side just behind the name "HOT-HEAD." Since the tank is from "A" Company, the name is obviously not related to the company letter. (USMC/NA)

**(Below)** During the recapture of Guam these M4A2s from the 2nd Separate Tank Company (STC) return from the front for resupply. They each have a geometric shape on their turret with a number in it, possibly to identify each tank platoon. (USMC/NA)

**(Above)** This M4A2 from the 2nd Separate Tank Company (STC) features a two-color camouflage pattern on it. The triangle on the side of the turret is probably a platoon tactical sign. The tank also has what appears to be wood planking on its side hull for protection against Japanese magnetic mines. (USMC/NA)

**(Below)** As amphibious warfare evolved, so did the markings for identification. Starting in the Marianas in the summer of 1944, colored stripes were frequently used on the hull sides of LVTs for beach placement. The single yellow stripe on the side of this LVT-2 denotes Yellow Beach 1. The tractor also carries a camouflage scheme that appears to be Olive Drab with a Tan overspray. (USMC/NA)

(Above) As the Marines moved up the Solomon Islands chain, camouflage became more common on their vehicles. This M3 75mm GMC being unloaded from an LST at Cape Gloucester carries an intricate camouflage pattern of Olive Drab, Brown, and Tan or Yellow. The crew has fitted a variety of machine guns in order to provide protection against Japanese infantry in the dense jungle. (USMC/NA)

(Below) A Marine swabs out the barrel of a camouflaged M4A1 on Cape Gloucester. The tank carries a pattern of Red Brown over its base coat of Olive Drab. Available information seems to indicate that the Marines did not have a general camouflage policy for patterns but left it up to the individual units. (USMC/NA)

(Above) This M3 75mm GMC carries a different type of camouflage pattern compared to the above M3. This scheme has broad bands of color and also features a cartoon emblem on the side. When combined with natural foliage and camouflage nets, such schemes proved very effective in the lush jungle growth encountered in the upper Solomons. (USMC/NA)

(Below) The M3A1s of the 3rd Marine Tank Battalion carried large numbers on a white panel on their turrets during the campaign on Bougainville. Many also had names and nudes on their hull sides. The tank is also equipped with extra fuel drums which were normally dropped before going into combat due to fire hazards. (USMC/NA)

(Above) Also at Tarawa was "C" Company of the 1st Corps' Medium Tank Battalion, composed of fourteen M4A2 Shermans. Each tank had a name beginning with "C," the company designation. On both sides of the hull was the battalion insignia, an elephant blowing smoke through its nose with a red blanket on its back. "COLORADO" was one of the few tanks to make it ashore. "COLORADO" was set ablaze by Japanese fire, but the crew drove it back to the beach and into the water to extinguish the flames. (USMC/NA)

(Above) "CHARLIE," from the 3rd Platoon, was knocked out after landing on Red Beach 3. The M4s carried a rack for water and fuel on the rear hull. All the names and elephant insignias were located just behind the first bogey wheel on the side of the hull. (USMC/NA)

(Below) The names and insignias were carried on both sides of the hull as seen here on "CONDOR," which was accidentally knocked out by a Navy Dauntless diver bomber. The Army serial number is barely visible just forward and above the name. All of the tanks were painted in Army Olive Drab (USMC/NA)

(Below) Besides the M4s, a number of M3A1s were also landed on Tarawa on the second and third days of the battle. These light tanks were from the 2nd Tank Battalion, the division tank unit. "COLUMBUS," from "C" Company, also carried a triangle on the turret side. The way it pointed indicated the company to which the tank was assigned. The tankers are wearing Marine camouflage fatigues just like their infantry counterparts. (USMC/NA)

(Above) As the war progressed up the Solomons, additional Marine armor was deployed to the Pacific. At Munda three Marine Defense Battalions employed small numbers of M3A1 light tanks. This trio of tanks from the 9th Defense Battalion advance near the Munda airfield in August 1943. The tanks are carrying Marine Corps serial numbers on their sides. These numbers appear to be somewhat oversized by comparison with Army serial numbers. The second tank also carries a name on its turret. (USA/NA)

### North Africa

The only instance in which Marines participated in an amphibious operation in the European Theater during World War II occurred in in November 1942 when a small number of LVT-1s were used during "Operation TORCH." These LVTs from the Atlantic Fleet Marine Force saw only limited service. They were painted Ocean Grey overall and were prominently marked with both stars and the American flag in the hopes the French would not fire on American troops.

(Below) Some LVTs, such as this LVT-2, had a large white panel painted on the driver's compartment with the battalion and vehicle number stenciled on it. The sides of the driver's compartment on the LVT-2 were smaller than that of the LVT-1 and less adaptable for markings. (USMC/NA)

(Above) The first use of amphibious tractors in the assault role was at Tarawa (Betio Atoll) in November 1943. Many of the LVTs had prominent numbers marked on the driver's compartment sides for identification purposes. This LVT-1 has had its markings, the number "28" and name "WHISKEY SOUR" roughly painted on in white. Most of the LVTs at Tarawa did not have names on them. (USMC/NA)

(Below) This LTV1, number "44," has had its numbers painted in a much neater manner than the previous photo. Most unusual is the upside-down star on the front of the driver's compartment. The LVTs used at Tarawa had additional armor bolted on the front and sides of the driver's compartment, but in spite of this added protection the 2nd Amphibious Tractor Battalion suffered a 65% casualty rate. All markings are in white while the LVT is in Ocean Gray. (USMC/NA)